Synergy Codes

The Alchemy of Meditation for Holistic Wellness Facilitators

Copyright © 2025 Chelsey Sarah Prusha
All rights reserved.

No part of this publication may be reproduced, stored in a retrieval system, or transmitted in any form or by any means—electronic, mechanical, photocopying, recording, or otherwise—without the prior written permission of the publisher, except in the case of brief quotations embodied in critical reviews or scholarly articles.

For permission requests or bulk orders, contact:
Synergy Wellness Collective
www.synergywellnesscollective.com
contactinfo.swc@gmail.com

Cover design, layout, and interior formatting by Camille Marie Rauscher.

ISBN: 979-8-9990769-1-5

This book is intended as a resource for wellness facilitators, meditation guides, energy healers, and holistic practitioners. It is not a substitute for medical, psychological, or psychiatric advice or treatment. Always consult qualified professionals when needed.

Dedication

To Joy Anderson —
the radiant soul who walked beside me as I entered the stillness for the very first time.

Our journey began in the classroom, where you opened my young mind to the unseen threads of human experience through the lens of sociology. What began as student and teacher soon expanded beyond time and title. You became my counselor, my hypnotherapist, my healer, my mentor, my colleague, my friend — my soul family.

You held sacred space for me long before I knew how to hold it for myself. You guided me inward when I only knew how to survive outwardly. You spoke the language of energy before I understood its rhythm — and through your presence, I came to understand that meditation isn't just a practice, but a portal to remembering who we truly are.

Thank you for walking with me across lifetimes — and especially in this one. This book is seeded with the wisdom you so generously shared, and it is offered in your honor.

With endless gratitude and deep love,
Chelsey

Table of Contents

Dedication 3
Introduction 6
   The Path Home Begins Within 7
Part I: Understanding Meditation 11
   What is Meditation? 12
   A Brief History of Meditation Across Cultures 16
   Science of Meditation 21
   The Layers of the Self 27
Part II: Categories of Meditation 32
   Mindfulness & Awareness-Based Practices 33
   Mantra & Sound-Based Practices 39
   Visualization & Hypnotic Practices 46
   Somatic & Energetic Meditations 52
   Spiritual Communion & Mystical Practices 58
   Earth & Elemental Connection Meditations 64
   Visual, Sacred Geometry & Fractal-Based Meditations 70
   Galactic & Ascension-Based Meditations 76
   Therapeutic & Trauma-Informed Practices 82
Part III: Creating & Facilitating Meditations 87
   Creating Meditations for Personal Practice 88

    Creating and Leading Meditations for Clients & Groups 92

    Designing General vs. Custom Meditations 97

Part IV: Integration & Embodiment........................ 102

    The Meditation Path as a Way of Life 103

    Becoming the Meditation 106

Appendix: Meditation Styles by Origin and Purpose. 111

    About the Author 118

Introduction

The Path Home Begins Within

Meditation didn't come to me in a yoga studio or a Himalayan cave. It found me in the aftermath — in the quiet ache after trauma, in the hollow of spiritual confusion, in the place where nothing else worked.

I came to meditation because I needed to survive. I stayed because I finally began to live.

Like many of us, I wasn't taught how to listen inwardly. I was taught to perform, to fix, to achieve, to obey. I was taught to suppress what felt too big, to medicate what didn't fit, to distrust the body and override the mind. But underneath it all, a deeper knowing stirred — a soul longing to be remembered.

Years after I first met Joy Anderson as my high school sociology teacher, our paths crossed again in a way I never could have predicted. At the time, I was deep in the trenches of my healing journey, working through complex PTSD and grappling with layers of trauma that traditional therapy alone couldn't reach. My therapist recommended I begin hypnotherapy to access the deeper roots of my pain — and referred me to someone she believed could guide me with both precision and compassion: Joy.

It was through the sacred container of hypnotherapy that I experienced meditation for the very first time. Not just as a practice — but as a gateway. A portal inward. A lifeline.

What began as a therapeutic process quickly evolved into something much more. Joy became more than a facilitator. She became my hypnotherapist, my healer, my mentor, my colleague, my friend, and my soul family. She was a midwife to the parts of me I didn't yet know how to love — the parts buried beneath trauma, shame, fear, and fragmentation. She helped me remember that stillness could be safe. That silence could be nourishing. That I could meet myself without needing to run away.

Since then, meditation has remained the single most transformative thread in my life. It has guided me through addiction, neurodivergent burnout, misdiagnosis, religious deconstruction, motherhood, grief, and spiritual rebirth. It gave me tools when I felt powerless. It gave me presence when I felt fractured. It gave me access to a part of myself that trauma could not erase — the eternal, sovereign, whole part. The part that always remembered.

Over the years, I've come to understand that meditation is not one thing. It is many things — a silence, a spiral, a sanctuary. A breath, a fire, a mirror. Meditation is prayer. It is science. It is ceremony. It is discipline, and it is surrender. It meets each of us exactly where we are and invites us into something deeper — not to escape this life, but to embody it more fully.

In a world of overstimulation, disconnection, and spiritual bypassing, meditation can become more than a practice — it can become a reclamation. A return to the body. A return to the Earth. A return to the soul's voice. A return to your Self.

This book is an offering born from my lived experience, clinical background, spiritual studies, and soul remembrance. It is a bridge between ancient traditions and modern applications. Between mystical transmission and grounded technique. Between your pain and your power.

Inside these pages, you will explore a wide spectrum of meditation styles from around the world — some rooted in centuries of wisdom, others emerging through new paradigms of healing and consciousness. You'll learn not just how to practice them, but how to create them — for yourself, for your clients, for your communities, and for the sacred future we are all building together.

Whether you are brand new to meditation or seeking to deepen your path, know this:

You do not need to be quiet to begin.

You do not need to be still to belong.

You only need to be willing —

To listen.

To breathe.

To remember.

Let us begin.

Part I: Understanding Meditation

What is Meditation?

A Return to the Sacred Within

Meditation is often spoken about as a tool, a technique, a way to calm the mind or relieve stress — and while those are valid expressions of its gifts, they only scratch the surface. At its essence, meditation is not something we do. It is a space we remember.

Meditation is a return.

A return to breath.

A return to presence.

A return to the part of you that is untouched by pain, story, or separation.

A return to your own divinity.

In a world that constantly pulls us outward — into stimulation, performance, fragmentation, and survival — meditation invites us inward. It is the art of listening. The practice of being with what is. It is the sacred act of turning toward the self with enough compassion, stillness, and curiosity that something deeper begins to emerge. That something is often called consciousness. Awareness. Spirit. Essence. But it has no true name — only the quiet recognition in your cells that you have come home.

Meditation is Not About Perfection

Despite popular belief, meditation is not about "clearing your mind" or sitting in lotus position on a mountaintop in perfect peace. It is not reserved for monks, yogis, or spiritual elites. Meditation is not about becoming someone else — it's about unlearning who you thought you had to be in order to survive. It's about remembering the wisdom already embedded in your breath, your body, your energy, your soul.

Some days, meditation may feel like a deep cosmic journey. Other days, it may feel like sitting with your anxiety and breathing through resistance. Both are valid. Both are healing. Both are sacred.

The Many Faces of Meditation

There is no one right way to meditate. In fact, as you'll explore throughout this book, meditation is as diverse as the human experience itself. From mantra repetition to sacred geometry, from candle gazing to breathwork, from trance journeys to silent presence — meditation takes many forms, each with its own purpose, rhythm, and energetic imprint.

Meditation can be still or moving.

It can be silent or sound-filled.

It can be ancient or emergent.

It can be structured or intuitive.

Whether you are sitting in zazen, walking barefoot on the earth, activating your DNA through light language, or simply closing your eyes to reconnect with your heart — you are meditating. You are tuning in. You are accessing the field of awareness that exists beneath the noise of thought and the pressure of doing.

A Living Practice

More than a technique, meditation is a way of relating to life. It is the choice to meet each moment with presence — to sit with grief, to listen to intuition, to open to beauty, to breathe through fear, to remember your wholeness when the world tries to convince you otherwise.

In this way, meditation becomes a companion. A living, breathing relationship with the Self. One that continues to evolve as you do.

And so, the question is not only What is meditation? but also:

What happens when I stop running from myself?

What emerges when I sit in the space between doing and being?

What wisdom has been waiting for me in the silence all along?

The answers will not come from me.

They will come from you —

From the still, sacred voice within you

That meditation has always known how to reach.

A Brief History of Meditation Across Cultures

Remembering the Roots of Inner Knowing
Meditation is not new. It is ancient — older than language, older than religion, older than time as we know it. It has been practiced in caves and temples, deserts and jungles, monasteries and mountaintops. It has been preserved in sacred texts and carried orally through lineages. It has been whispered through breath, encoded in geometry, and offered in silence.

Meditation is humanity's original medicine.

Long before modern science began to measure its effects on the brain or the nervous system, our ancestors understood the necessity of stillness, contemplation, and communion with the unseen. They knew that by turning inward, one could access something sacred — not just for personal peace, but for collective harmony. Meditation was not a self-help strategy. It was a spiritual discipline, a soul technology, a way to stay aligned with creation.

What follows is not an exhaustive history, but an honoring — a remembrance of how diverse cultures across the world have cultivated inner awareness in their own sacred ways.

India: The Birthplace of Formal Meditation

The earliest written records of meditation come from the Vedas, ancient spiritual texts from India dating back over 5,000 years. These texts introduced dhyana — a form of focused attention — as part of an eight-limbed yogic path toward union with the divine.

Meditation evolved through Hindu traditions into various schools of Raja Yoga, Tantra, and Vedanta, all emphasizing the subtle body, mantras, breathwork (pranayama), and higher states of consciousness. These practices were designed not to escape the body but to integrate it as a vessel for enlightenment.

Later, Buddhism emerged from this spiritual soil, bringing new forms of meditation such as Vipassana (insight meditation) and Metta (loving-kindness). The Buddha taught meditation as a path to liberation — a way to witness the impermanence of all things and dissolve the ego's grasp on suffering.

China and Taoist Lineages

In China, Taoist meditation focused on cultivating internal energy (Qi) and aligning with nature's rhythms. Practices like Qi Gong, Zuo Wang (sitting in forgetfulness), and the Microcosmic Orbit emphasized flow, inner harmony, and the transmutation of dense emotion into pure life force.

These traditions deeply influenced Chan Buddhism — which later evolved into Zen in Japan — known for its stark simplicity and the power of silent sitting (zazen) as a mirror to one's true nature.

Indigenous and Earth-Based Traditions

Indigenous cultures across the globe have long practiced meditative states, though they may not have used the term "meditation." These were rituals of presence, sacred observation, and spiritual journeying. In North and South American traditions, shamanic journeying facilitated contact with spirit guides, ancestors, and alternate realms of healing.

In African and Aboriginal Australian cultures, trance states were accessed through drumming, dance, and elemental communion. These meditations were communal and embodied, grounded in a deep relationship with land, animal spirits, and cosmic time.

Middle Eastern and Mystical Traditions

In Jewish Kabbalah, meditation involved contemplation on the Hebrew letters, divine names, and the Tree of Life. These practices were seen as direct methods to unify with the Source and illuminate the soul.

Christian Mysticism gave rise to contemplative prayer and the sacred silence of monastic life. Figures like Teresa of Ávila, John of the Cross, and the Desert Fathers and Mothers used meditation to enter direct union with God through love, stillness, and surrender.

Islamic Sufism developed practices like dhikr (remembrance of God) and whirling to induce ecstatic states. These meditations emphasized heart purification, divine love, and losing oneself in the Beloved.

Modern and Western Adaptations
In the 20th century, meditation spread rapidly to the West, largely through teachers who brought Eastern philosophies into new contexts. Pioneers like Swami Vivekananda, Paramahansa Yogananda, and Thich Nhat Hanh helped bridge these ancient teachings with modern seekers.

By the 1970s, practices like Transcendental Meditation and Mindfulness-Based Stress Reduction (MBSR) became mainstream, introducing meditation to healthcare, psychology, and education. These adaptations emphasized clinical benefits — stress reduction, emotional balance, cognitive focus — without always retaining the full spiritual frameworks.

While these simplified approaches helped make meditation accessible, they also highlighted a growing need for re-sacralizing the practice — for remembering its roots in reverence, not just relaxation.

A Living Tradition, Not a Fixed Method
Across all these traditions, one truth remains: meditation is not a single technique. It is a living lineage — a multidimensional relationship with life, Spirit, and the Self. It evolves with culture, yet never loses its essence. Every era, every people, every soul brings something new to its unfolding.

This book honors the depth and diversity of those lineages. It also acknowledges that the practice of meditation is no longer bound to temples or texts alone — it now lives in the breath of a mother finding peace after trauma, in the heart of a neurodivergent child learning to regulate, in the voice of a healer guiding others into stillness.

Meditation is yours.
It belongs to all.
And in honoring its roots, we ensure its wings.

Science of Meditation

Brainwaves, Nervous System, and Healing
While meditation is often experienced as a spiritual or emotional practice, it is also a deeply physiological one. In fact, modern neuroscience is finally beginning to confirm what ancient traditions have always known: when we change our internal state, we change our reality.

Meditation is not just about sitting still. It's about rewiring the brain, recalibrating the nervous system, and reactivating the body's innate ability to heal itself.

This chapter explores the biology behind the stillness — the measurable shifts that occur in the brain, body, and energy field when we enter meditative states. Whether you're a seeker or a skeptic, understanding the science of meditation offers a profound validation: you are not imagining the changes. You are embodying them.

Brainwaves: The Language of Consciousness
Our brains operate through electrical impulses that generate distinct patterns, known as brainwaves. Each wave reflects a different state of consciousness and serves a unique function in our mental, emotional, and energetic processing.

Beta (13–30 Hz)

The fast-paced, alert state of ordinary waking consciousness. Associated with thinking, analyzing, decision-making, and often — stress. Most people spend the majority of their day in high beta, especially when multitasking or operating in survival mode.

Alpha (8–12 Hz)

The bridge between thinking and being. Alpha waves arise in light relaxation — such as daydreaming, gentle reflection, or entering a meditative flow. They are associated with creative insight, ease, and integration.

Theta (4–8 Hz)

The realm of deep meditation, trance, hypnosis, and dream-like states. Theta opens access to the subconscious mind, where memories, emotions, and archetypal imagery reside. Healing, reprogramming, and deep emotional processing often happen here.

Delta (0.5–4 Hz)

The slowest waves, associated with deep, restorative sleep and unconscious healing. Some advanced meditation or yogic nidra states can access delta while awake, allowing cellular regeneration and nervous system repair.

Gamma (30-100 Hz)

Linked with heightened states of perception, bliss, unity consciousness, and integration across both hemispheres of the brain. Experienced in moments of peak intuition, spiritual awakening, or deep compassion. Some advanced meditators (e.g., Tibetan monks) sustain gamma during prolonged states of meditation.

When you meditate, you're not just relaxing — you're shifting your brain's operating system. Regular practice increases alpha and theta activity, enhances neuroplasticity, and allows conscious access to subconscious patterning. This is how we change not only how we feel, but how we *function*.

The Nervous System: From Survival to Safety
The autonomic nervous system (ANS) governs our body's automatic responses, including stress, rest, and digestion. It has two primary branches:

Sympathetic Nervous System (SNS) - The "fight, flight, or freeze" response. Activated in perceived danger or stress. In chronic trauma or dysregulation, the SNS becomes overactive — leading to anxiety, hypervigilance, sleep disturbances, or burnout.

Parasympathetic Nervous System (PNS) - The "rest and digest" or "heal and repair" system. Activated in states of safety, presence, and connection. This is where the body restores balance, heals tissue, and releases stored trauma.

Meditation, especially when paired with breathwork or somatic awareness, gently deactivates the sympathetic system and strengthens parasympathetic response. Over time, this retrains the body to recognize safety, regulate emotions, and re-establish internal coherence.

Polyvagal Theory, developed by Dr. Stephen Porges, expands this understanding by highlighting the role of the vagus nerve, a key player in the body's social, emotional, and immune responses. Through meditation, vagal tone improves — enhancing resilience, empathy, digestion, and overall wellbeing.

Healing Effects of Meditation: Evidence-Based Benefits

Modern research supports what spiritual lineages have long practiced. Here are some of the most well-documented effects of meditation:

- Reduces stress and cortisol levels
- Lowers blood pressure and heart rate

- Improves focus, memory, and cognitive function
- Enhances immune system response
- Decreases symptoms of anxiety, depression, and PTSD
- Increases gray matter in regions related to self-awareness and compassion
- Promotes emotional regulation and nervous system resilience
- Supports trauma integration and recovery

Meditation doesn't bypass the body — it brings us back to it. Back to presence. Back to power. Back to the place where healing becomes possible not because we force it, but because we *allow* it.

Meditation as a Multidimensional Healing Tool

While science gives us language for what happens in the physical brain and body, meditation also opens access to realms beyond measurement — the energetic, the emotional, the spiritual, the ancestral, and the quantum.

In hypnotherapy, for example, we move through theta states to reach stored imprints from childhood, past lives, or soul contracts. In energy work, meditation aligns us with subtle body systems and bioelectric coherence. In spiritual practice, meditation is the gateway to the Higher Self, the Akashic field, divine communion, or cosmic consciousness.

These layers may not all be visible under a brain scan, but they are felt — and they are real.

You Are the Healer, the Receiver, and the Field
Meditation reminds us that healing is not something done *to* us — it is something awakened *within* us. Every breath, every moment of mindful presence, every inner journey reclaims part of the self that was once lost, dissociated, or silenced.

Whether you're looking to rewire your neural pathways, calm your heart rate, reclaim your intuition, or connect with your soul's wisdom — meditation is a doorway. It meets you at the intersection of spirit and science. Of stillness and transformation. Of survival and sacred embodiment.

And every time you choose to sit, to breathe, to witness, to remember —
You are choosing to return.

The Layers of the Self

Body, Mind, Spirit & Energy Field
You are not just a body.
You are not just a mind.
You are not just a soul.
You are a symphony — a layered, living system of intelligence and energy that spans the physical and the metaphysical.

To truly understand meditation, we must understand *who* it is that meditates. Not just the person sitting on the cushion, but the vast multidimensional being they are — and always have been. Meditation is not simply about calming the mind. It is about bringing coherence to the layers of your being — integrating the scattered fragments into one sacred whole.

In this chapter, we'll explore these primary layers: the body, the mind, the spirit, and the energy field — how they interact, how they influence your lived experience, and how meditation weaves them back into alignment.

The Physical Body: The Temple
The body is the most visible and tangible layer of the self — your sacred vessel, your living temple. It holds your history, your instincts, your emotions, your trauma, and your wisdom. It does not lie. It speaks in sensation, in tension, in impulse, and in pain or pleasure.

Many people come to meditation because their bodies are screaming for relief — from stress, from inflammation, from fatigue, from the cumulative impact of unprocessed experience.

Through meditation, we bring awareness *into* the body. We begin to listen. We soften the bracing. We breathe into tightness. We reinhabit the skin we've been taught to escape. And over time, the body responds — not by forgetting pain, but by reorganizing around presence and safety.

When you meditate with your body, you restore your relationship with the earth. With the now. With your own primal truth.

The Mind: The Storykeeper

The mind is a powerful tool — a storyteller, protector, analyzer, and meaning-maker. It houses both the conscious thoughts you're aware of and the vast subconscious patterns that operate in the background.

The mind is often what people think they must "quiet" in order to meditate. But the truth is: the goal is not to *erase* thoughts. The goal is to *witness* them — to detach from their grip and recognize that you are not your thoughts. You are the one who sees them.

The mind can become fragmented by trauma, overstimulation, or unintegrated beliefs. Meditation helps soften its rigid loops, unravel distorted narratives, and build new neural pathways rooted in clarity and compassion.

In hypnotic or guided states, we can access the subconscious mind, where old programming lives — and begin to update those scripts, inviting healing at a root level.

When you meditate with your mind, you rewrite your inner narrative and open the doorway to deep transformation.

The Spirit: The Eternal Self
Beyond the body and the mind is the spirit — your essence, your soul, your spark of divine intelligence. This is the part of you that existed before this life and will continue long after. It is not bound by form. It remembers why you came here.

The spirit is often experienced as intuition, love, inner knowing, or presence. In deep meditative states, we attune to this level — entering union with the Higher Self, the divine, or the infinite field of awareness. For some, this feels like light. For others, a sense of deep homecoming or unconditional peace.

Spirit doesn't require dogma or religion. It only requires space — and your willingness to listen.

When you meditate with your spirit, you remember who you truly are. You reconnect to your purpose. You return to love.

The Energy Field: The Invisible Matrix

Surrounding and permeating all layers of the self is your energy field — the multidimensional electromagnetic matrix that records, transmits, and processes information far beyond what the five senses perceive.

Often referred to as the aura, biofield, or light body, this layer includes your chakras, meridians, auric layers, and soul codes. It is sensitive to internal emotion and external stimuli — other people's energy, environmental frequencies, planetary shifts, and collective consciousness.

Your energy field stores the unspoken: ancestral patterns, karmic residue, soul contracts, and suppressed emotion. It reflects the state of your nervous system, thoughts, and spirit in real time.

Meditation helps you cleanse, stabilize, and recalibrate this field. Practices such as light visualization, chakra alignment, breathwork, or sacred geometry work on this level — restoring energetic coherence and vibrational alignment.

When you meditate with your energy field, you move from surviving to resonating. You become a clear channel for your own soul frequency.

The body holds.
The mind remembers.

The spirit guides.
The energy field reflects.

When all of these aspects are disconnected, we feel disoriented, dysregulated, and disempowered. But when they come into alignment — through intentional practice, breath, and presence — we become integrated. Sovereign. Whole.

Meditation is the unifier. It is the space in which all these layers meet, speak, heal, and realign. It doesn't ask you to choose between science and soul, thought and feeling, seen and unseen. It asks only that you show up — fully — and listen.

Because you are not just one thing.
You are many layers, vibrating as one.

And you are ready to come home.

Part II: Categories of Meditation

Mindfulness & Awareness-Based Practices

The Art of Being with What Is
At the heart of nearly every meditation tradition lies the invitation to *become aware* — not of something lofty or esoteric, but of this very moment. Of your breath, your body, your thoughts, your sensations. Of what is unfolding *now*.

Mindfulness and awareness-based meditation practices are foundational tools for inner transformation. They require no specific beliefs, no special tools, no rituals — only your willingness to notice, without judgment, what is already here. These practices reconnect us with the raw truth of our experience and train the nervous system to soften into presence rather than react to stress, pain, or discomfort.

Below are four cornerstone practices in this category, each offering a unique lens into mindful awareness.

Vipassana (Insight Meditation)
Vipassana is one of the oldest forms of meditation, dating back over 2,500 years to the teachings of Siddhartha Gautama, the Buddha. The word *Vipassana* means "clear seeing" or "insight" in Pali. It is the practice of observing reality as it truly is — not through the mind's stories, but through direct sensory experience.

Rooted in the Theravāda Buddhist tradition, Vipassana was preserved in monastic lineages throughout Southeast Asia, and was brought to the West primarily through teachers like S.N. Goenka, who taught large silent retreats in the tradition of Sayagyi U Ba Khin.

The technique centers on bare attention — cultivating sustained observation of bodily sensations, thoughts, emotions, and breath, without trying to change or control them. Through this non-reactive awareness, practitioners begin to see the impermanence (*anicca*), unsatisfactoriness (*dukkha*), and non-self (*anatta*) nature of all phenomena.

The benefits of Vipassana are profound. It builds emotional resilience, reduces reactivity, and creates a spacious inner witness who can hold pain, fear, or joy without collapsing into them. Long-term practice supports spiritual insight, trauma healing, and deep mental purification.

Vipassana is typically practiced in silence, in stillness, and often in retreat settings. Yet its power lies in its simplicity — the radical act of being with what is.

Zazen (Zen Meditation)
Zazen, meaning "seated meditation" in Japanese, is the core practice of Zen Buddhism, which developed as a fusion of Indian Mahāyāna Buddhism and Chinese Taoist thought, known originally as Chan in

China. Zen was later transmitted to Japan by masters like Dōgen Zenji in the 13th century.

Unlike other practices that may use breath or mantra as a focal point, Zazen emphasizes *just sitting* — resting in pure awareness without grasping at thoughts or chasing sensations. It is the embodiment of *shikantaza*, or "nothing but sitting." In some traditions, Zazen includes koan practice, in which paradoxical riddles are contemplated to break the habitual logic of the egoic mind.

Zazen is traditionally practiced facing a wall, with upright posture, half-lotus or kneeling, in silence. The practitioner doesn't try to stop thoughts but instead notices them arising and passing, like clouds across the sky. There is no agenda, no striving — only presence.

The purpose of Zazen is not self-improvement, but self-emptying. It is a gateway to ego dissolution, to experiencing the inherent emptiness and interconnection of all things. Over time, Zazen cultivates deep inner stillness, mental clarity, non-attachment, and what Zen calls "beginner's mind" — a pure, open, receptive state.

More than a technique, Zazen is a way of being. It invites us to drop beneath striving and simply dwell in the truth of the moment, exactly as it is.

Mindfulness-Based Stress Reduction (MBSR)

MBSR is a secular, science-backed meditation program developed in the late 1970s by Dr. Jon Kabat-Zinn at the University of Massachusetts Medical Center. Blending elements of Vipassana, Hatha Yoga, and body-based awareness, MBSR was designed to bring the healing power of mindfulness to clinical settings, especially for patients suffering from chronic pain, anxiety, depression, and stress-related conditions.

The core definition of mindfulness in this context is: *"paying attention in a particular way — on purpose, in the present moment, and non-judgmentally."* This simple orientation radically transforms how we relate to our inner and outer experience.

The standard MBSR program lasts eight weeks and includes practices such as the body scan, sitting meditation, gentle yoga, and mindful movement. Participants learn to observe thoughts and emotions without clinging to them or pushing them away, developing what's called *decentered awareness* — the ability to witness without being consumed.

MBSR is unique in its emphasis on embodiment and self-regulation. Rather than seeking transcendence, it empowers people to stay present with the discomforts of life — and to relate to suffering with curiosity rather than avoidance.

The program has been studied extensively and shows measurable improvements in mood regulation, immune function, brain plasticity, and pain tolerance. It has become a foundational model for therapeutic mindfulness around the world.

For many, MBSR is a gateway into meditation — one that demystifies the process and provides accessible, scientifically validated tools for wellbeing.

Walking Meditation
While seated practices are often emphasized in meditation traditions, walking meditation offers a powerful alternative — especially for those who are neurodivergent, somatically sensitive, or find stillness overstimulating.

Walking meditation has been practiced in Buddhist monasteries for centuries, used as a bridge between sitting sessions. The most well-known teacher to popularize it in the West is Thích Nhất Hạnh, the beloved Vietnamese Zen master who taught that *"peace is every step."*

In walking meditation, the practitioner brings mindful attention to each footstep, breath, and body movement. The pace is often slow and intentional, though it can also be adapted to natural or brisk walking. The key is to be fully present — not walking to get somewhere, but walking to *be* somewhere.

Each step becomes a mantra. Each breath, a prayer. Distractions are met with gentle noticing, and the rhythm of movement becomes the anchor for awareness.

Walking meditation reconnects us to grounded presence, engages the vestibular system, and soothes the nervous system. It is especially powerful in natural environments, where earth-based meditation meets ecological consciousness.

This practice teaches that we do not need silence to be still, nor stillness to be aware. We carry mindfulness wherever we go — with our soles and with our soul.

Mindfulness and awareness-based practices offer more than relaxation — they offer liberation. Liberation from unconscious reactivity, from inherited stories, from the trance of autopilot living. They teach us to sit with ourselves, to walk with presence, and to witness without grasping.

Whether you begin with the ancient insight of Vipassana, the stark simplicity of Zazen, the therapeutic tools of MBSR, or the gentle rhythm of walking meditation — you are entering a lineage of presence. One that asks nothing more, and nothing less, than your full attention.

Because awareness is not just something we practice. It's something we become.

Mantra & Sound-Based Practices

The Healing Power of Vibration and Voice
If awareness is the stillness of meditation, then sound is its pulse.

Long before language was formed, sound was medicine. Vibration was a bridge between realms. The ancient ones knew that sound was not merely auditory — it was energetic. It moved through the cells, through the chakras, through the auric field. It shaped matter and consciousness. In nearly every spiritual tradition across time, sound has been used to invoke healing, connect with the divine, activate sacred memory, and entrain the mind into deeper states of being.

Mantra and sound-based meditations are practices of resonance. They use vibration — spoken, sung, whispered, or silently repeated — to alter the inner landscape. Whether it's a Sanskrit mantra, a sacred syllable, a devotional song, or a rhythmic chant, each repetition becomes a tuning fork for the soul.

Below are five powerful expressions of this sacred sound lineage.

Mantra Meditation (Vedic)
The word *mantra* comes from Sanskrit: *man* meaning "mind" and *tra* meaning "tool" or "instrument." A mantra, then, is a tool of the mind — not to control it, but to liberate it.

Vedic Mantra Meditation originates from ancient India, deeply rooted in the *Rig Veda*, one of the oldest spiritual texts on Earth. In this tradition, mantras are not just affirmations — they are living frequencies, each with a specific vibrational signature and spiritual purpose. Repeating a mantra aligns the practitioner's energy field with the divine archetype or universal principle it represents.

Some mantras invoke specific deities (like *Om Namah Shivaya* for Shiva), while others serve broader purposes, such as *So Hum* ("I am that") or the universal seed sound *Om*, said to be the sound of creation itself.

The repetition — either out loud (*vaikhari*), whispered (*upamsu*), or silent (*manasika*) — creates a rhythm in the body and nervous system. Over time, the mantra penetrates the subconscious mind, dissolving distraction and anchoring the practitioner in pure awareness.

Mantra meditation supports emotional regulation, concentration, spiritual attunement, and energetic purification. It's also accessible to those who struggle with silent meditation, offering a tangible anchor for the wandering mind.

Transcendental Meditation (TM)
Transcendental Meditation, or TM, is a modern system of mantra-based meditation developed by Maharishi Mahesh Yogi and introduced to the West

in the 1950s and 60s — famously adopted by the Beatles and other cultural figures seeking expanded consciousness.

While it draws from ancient Vedic knowledge, TM is structured for accessibility. Practitioners are given a personalized mantra — typically a bija (seed) sound — by a certified teacher. The practice involves sitting comfortably for 20 minutes twice a day, silently repeating the mantra in a relaxed, effortless manner.

The purpose of TM is to allow the mind to "transcend" thought — to drop into a state beyond thinking, beyond doing, into a field of restful alertness and pure being. It's not about concentration or control, but natural descent into the source of thought — often referred to as *the Unified Field* or *pure consciousness.*

Scientific research on TM has shown consistent benefits: reduced cortisol levels, improved focus, enhanced creativity, and deep nervous system recovery. It's often described as achieving the rest of deep sleep while remaining awake.

TM is especially useful for high-performing or anxious minds that benefit from a repetitive, sound-based anchor — and it opens a gateway to effortless presence without force.

Chanting (OM, Seed Sounds, Sacred Languages)
Chanting bridges mantra and breath. It calls the

vibration into the body — not just as a whisper in the mind, but as a resonance that moves through bone, blood, and breath.

Perhaps the most recognizable chant in the world is OM, known in Sanskrit as the *primordial sound* or *cosmic hum* — said to be the vibrational seed of the universe itself. OM (or AUM) is often chanted at the beginning or end of a practice to ground, cleanse, and open the field to divine presence.

Beyond OM, there are countless bija mantras — seed syllables that correspond to chakras and elemental energies. For example:

- *Lam* for the root chakra (earth)
- *Vam* for the sacral chakra (water)
- *Ram* for the solar plexus (fire)
- *Yam* for the heart (air)
- *Ham* for the throat (ether)
- *Om* for the third eye
- *Aum* or silence for the crown

In addition, many traditions use sacred languages like Sanskrit, Hebrew, Aramaic, and Latin — not for their semantic meaning, but for their vibrational power. Chanting in these languages can activate archetypal memory, ancestral lineages, or soul codes long dormant.

Chanting strengthens breath control, harmonizes brain hemispheres, stimulates vagal tone, and awakens deep states of devotion. It's a practice of both sound and silence — for in the echo of a chant, the quiet speaks loudest.

Sufi Dhikr

In Sufism, the mystical branch of Islam, sound and breath become portals to union with the Divine. One of its most sacred practices is Dhikr (or *Zikr*), which means "remembrance." The purpose is simple: to remember God — not as a concept, but as a living presence.

Dhikr is performed through rhythmic repetition of divine names — such as *Allah*, *Al-Haqq* (The Truth), *Al-Wadud* (The Loving), or *La ilaha illa'llah* ("There is no god but God"). It may be done silently, whispered, or chanted aloud — individually or in community.

Over time, the repetition becomes internalized, like a heartbeat. The practitioner is not simply saying the names of God, but *becoming* the vibration of those names. In this way, dhikr dissolves the illusion of separation and opens the heart to ecstatic communion.

Physiologically, it induces trance states, balances the nervous system, and purifies emotional density. Spiritually, it grounds the practitioner in humility, love, and surrender. Though rooted in Islamic devotion, dhikr can be appreciated as a universal path of resonance, reverence, and embodied praise.

Kirtan & Devotional Song

Kirtan is the joyous expression of Bhakti Yoga — the yoga of devotion. Originating in India, kirtan involves call-and-response singing of sacred mantras, often accompanied by harmonium, drums, and dancing. The purpose is not performance, but devotional communion.

Chants often invoke divine archetypes or deities — such as Krishna, Durga, Hanuman, Shiva, or the Divine Mother — with each name representing a different aspect of universal consciousness. The repetition, rhythm, and group resonance create an emotional crescendo that opens the heart.

Unlike silent meditation, kirtan is extroverted — it moves energy *through* you. It allows grief to move, joy to swell, and love to overflow. In a world that suppresses the voice, kirtan liberates it.

Devotional singing also exists in many spiritual traditions — from Gospel music, to Gregorian chant, to Hawaiian oli, to medicine songs of the Amazon. Across cultures, song is soul-language — a way to speak to the sacred when words fall short.

Energetically, kirtan recalibrates the heart chakra, moves stuck emotion, builds community, and opens the energetic channel of the throat. It teaches us that sound is not just to be heard — it is to be felt, embodied, and shared.

Sound-based meditation is not just heard — it is *lived*. It invites you to *vibrate* at the frequency of the sacred, to use your voice as a tuning fork for healing, devotion, and awakening. Whether through the silent echo of a mantra, the rhythmic pulse of dhikr, or the joyful roar of kirtan — you are remembering your birthright: to *resonate* with the universe.

You are not separate from the sacred sound.
You *are* the sacred sound.

Visualization & Hypnotic Practices

Awakening the Inner Landscape
The imagination is not a form of escape — it is a gateway to the subconscious, the soul, and the multidimensional self. Visualization and hypnotic meditation practices use the mind's inner eye not to drift into fantasy, but to reshape inner reality from the inside out. These practices invite the practitioner to travel inward — into story, symbol, archetype, sensation, and energy. They speak the language of the subconscious: images, emotions, and metaphor. By engaging this realm, we gain access not only to buried memories and psychological material, but also to ancient wisdom, future timelines, soul fragments, and transformational codes.

Unlike passive or breath-focused meditations, these are guided journeys — crafted intentionally to lead the listener into expanded states of consciousness where healing, reprogramming, and soul retrieval can occur. Each journey is a co-creation between facilitator and seeker, where the landscape is both deeply personal and universally archetypal.

Guided Imagery & Visualization
Guided imagery is one of the most accessible and versatile forms of meditation. It typically involves listening to a recorded or live voice that paints a mental journey — through forest paths, celestial temples, inner sanctuaries, or mythic landscapes — designed to evoke healing, inspiration, or transformation. Unlike abstract mindfulness

practices, guided visualizations offer a clear, structured experience that engages the inner senses and keeps the mind gently focused.

The roots of this practice are cross-cultural. It draws upon ancient shamanic journeying, Jungian active imagination, Vedic visualization, and even contemporary therapeutic methods and performance psychology. From mystics and medicine men to athletes and trauma therapists, visualization has long been recognized as a powerful tool for transformation.

The brain responds to vividly imagined experiences as if they were real, triggering corresponding emotional and physiological shifts. This makes guided visualization especially effective for stress relief, energy healing, nervous system regulation, and manifestation. These practices can guide energy to specific organs, chakras, or memories, support emotional catharsis, and activate inner resources or archetypes. They are particularly supportive for beginners, neurodivergent individuals, and those recovering from trauma — offering a vivid, structured, and non-threatening container for healing.

Yoga Nidra
Yoga Nidra, often translated as "yogic sleep," is a deeply restorative practice that invites the practitioner to rest in the liminal state between waking and sleep — a space where the subconscious opens and the body releases held tension at its deepest layers. Rooted in Tantric teachings and formalized by Swami Satyananda Saraswati in the

mid-20th century, Yoga Nidra has gained global recognition for its profound healing effects.

The structure typically begins with the practitioner lying in savasana (corpse pose), followed by a systematic body scan, breath awareness, the setting of a sankalpa (heart-centered intention), and visualizations of archetypal or symbolic imagery. The practitioner remains consciously aware while the body enters a parasympathetic state of healing — where brainwaves shift into delta and theta frequencies.

Yoga Nidra is not about effort or mental control. It is about surrender — allowing the mind to soften, the body to restore, and the soul to speak through images, feelings, and silence. It is especially powerful for releasing trauma, regulating sleep, balancing hormones, and accessing higher guidance. In this receptive space, the sankalpa (intention) is planted in the fertile ground of the subconscious, where it can grow into embodied change.

Hypnotherapy Journeys
Hypnotherapy-based meditations combine the depth of hypnosis with the spaciousness of guided visualization, offering a direct path to the subconscious mind for healing and reprogramming. As a certified clinical and multidimensional hypnotherapist, I understand this method as both an art and a sacred technology — one that meets the

seeker in their core stories, inner wounds, and soul contracts.

Hypnotherapy is not mind control. It is a gentle induction into focused relaxation, typically accompanied by deepening techniques like descending stairs, entering a sacred room, or connecting with a trusted guide. Once the subconscious opens, the journey may involve regression, symbolic healing, reparenting, or energetic clearing. Each session ends with positive affirmations or integration techniques that support sustainable transformation.

These meditations are effective for rewriting limiting beliefs, integrating trauma, releasing ancestral burdens, activating purpose, and even accessing past lives or multidimensional selves. Because they are guided with intentional structure, they can reach root-level material that more passive forms of meditation may bypass. In this altered state, clients often experience emotional catharsis, physical release, deep knowing, and alignment with their higher path.

Inner Child & Future Self Journeys
Two of the most impactful guided meditation tools in the subconscious healing toolkit are inner child and future self journeys. These practices transcend time, allowing us to connect with earlier or evolved aspects of ourselves in a safe, nurturing space.

Inner child meditation involves journeying back to a younger version of yourself — often one who experienced neglect, trauma, or disconnection. This younger self is met with compassion, protection, and care. You become your own guide, reparenting the inner child in a way that your past environment may not have been able to. These journeys allow the body to release stored trauma, the nervous system to find a new baseline of safety, and the psyche to feel seen and integrated.

Future self meditations, on the other hand, bring you into resonance with the version of yourself who has already healed, grown, and embodied your soul's purpose. This self may appear in a visionary space — radiant, wise, and clear — offering guidance, emotional support, or energetic upgrades. By connecting with this timeline, you activate the vibration of what is already possible and allow it to ripple into your present reality.

Both of these journey types are deeply soul-integrative. They realign fragmented aspects of the self into wholeness and foster coherence across time. They are especially useful in coaching, hypnotherapy, shadow work, and identity reconstruction — helping the practitioner bridge the gap between who they've been, who they are, and who they are becoming.

Visualization and hypnotic meditations remind us that the mind is not the enemy — it is the paintbrush of creation. When focused with intention and supported by sacred guidance, it becomes a channel for healing, integration, and divine remembering. These practices do not require silence. They require presence. A willingness to journey into the sacred stories written within the soul.

To visualize is to reclaim authorship over your inner world.
To journey is to remember that your healing is not linear — it is symbolic, cyclical, and deeply alive.
And in this remembering, you awaken not only insight, but transformation — one image, one breath, one sacred scene at a time.

Somatic & Energetic Meditations

The Body as Portal, the Energy Field as Language
Meditation is not limited to the mind — it is also a deep practice of the body, breath, and the subtle rivers of life force that flow within and beyond the physical form. Somatic and energetic meditation styles remind us that our bodies are not obstacles to enlightenment — they are the doorway. Every cell, every sensation, every rhythmic pulse of breath is a gateway into presence, healing, and soul-level integration.

Somatic meditation grounds awareness into the felt sense. It teaches us to inhabit our body as wise, to perceive sensation not as distraction but as communication. Energetic meditation expands this awareness into the subtle body — the chakras, meridians, organs, and aura. Together, they dissolve the perceived boundary between form and spirit, returning us to the living reality of embodiment as sacred.

Let's explore four foundational methods that awaken the inner flow of energy and deepen our relationship with the body as temple.

Chakra Meditation
Chakra meditation is one of the most recognized forms of energetic meditation, focusing on the primary energy centers aligned along the spine. Traditionally there are seven chakras, each corresponding to a color, sound, element, gland, and

psychological archetype. However, in advanced systems such as Rainbow Reiki, we acknowledge additional centers — expanding into twelve, sixteen, or even eighteen chakras — connecting with galactic and multidimensional aspects of self.

Each chakra reflects a unique theme. The Root (Muladhara) connects us to stability and ancestral grounding. The Sacral (Svadhisthana) holds our emotional currents and creative sensuality. The Solar Plexus (Manipura) awakens personal power, self-worth, and identity. The Heart (Anahata) opens compassion, forgiveness, and the sacred bridge between Earth and Spirit. The Throat (Vishuddha) governs authentic expression and voice. The Third Eye (Ajna) reveals intuition, clarity, and vision. And the Crown (Sahasrara) dissolves separation, allowing unity with the Divine.

Chakra meditation might involve visualizing a colored vortex of energy at each center, chanting the associated bija mantra (such as "Lam" for the root, "Yam" for the heart), breathing into tension or spaciousness in each area, or sensing where blockages, stagnation, or vitality are present. As awareness deepens, one may experience expanded states of consciousness, spontaneous healing, or emotional releases.

Advanced chakra work includes light code transmission, ancestral clearing, trauma integration, and spiritual activation. It is not just about balancing — it is about attuning to the full spectrum of one's energetic intelligence. Each chakra becomes a doorway into wholeness, and through that doorway, we remember our soul's architecture.

Kundalini Practices
Kundalini is the name for the dormant spiritual energy said to lie coiled at the base of the spine, like a serpent waiting to awaken. When activated, this energy rises through the sushumna nadi — the central channel — piercing and purifying each chakra as it ascends toward the crown. The experience can be transformative, even life-changing.

Kundalini practices are designed to gently awaken and channel this energy. These meditations often include pranayama (breathwork), mudras (hand gestures), mantras, and specific sequences of movement known as kriyas. These kriyas are not arbitrary — they are energetically calibrated to clear blocks, detoxify the body, and elevate consciousness.

Popularized in the West through the teachings of Yogi Bhajan, Kundalini Yoga incorporates these techniques to build inner heat, strengthen the nervous system, and elevate awareness. The goal is not just physical health, but spiritual awakening.

Energetically, Kundalini work clears stagnation and trauma stored in the chakras and aura, expands perception, activates intuitive gifts, and accelerates soul remembrance. However, because of its intensity, this practice should be approached with reverence and proper grounding. When facilitated safely, Kundalini meditation becomes a divine current —

burning away illusion, illuminating truth, and resurrecting the higher self within.

Qi Gong Meditation
Qi Gong is a sacred movement and meditation system rooted in Taoist philosophy and traditional Chinese medicine. Translated as "life force cultivation," Qi Gong integrates posture, movement, breath, and visualization to harmonize Qi — the vital energy that animates all life.

Qi Gong meditations are both physical and energetic. The movements are slow and intentional, designed not to exhaust the body, but to nourish it. Practitioners often begin by centering at the dantian, the energetic reservoir located just below the navel. From there, breath and awareness are guided through the body's meridian pathways, unblocking stagnant Qi and restoring natural flow.

Qi Gong also includes standing meditations, where the practitioner holds a posture (such as "embracing the tree") while directing awareness through specific energetic gates. Some meditations are done seated or lying down, focusing on inner alchemy — transforming energy within the organs and connecting Heaven and Earth.

Spiritually, Qi Gong opens the practitioner to the Tao — the Great Way — not through concept, but through embodied resonance. It improves immunity, calms the mind, strengthens the organs, and balances masculine and feminine polarities. This practice reminds us that movement can be meditation, and stillness can be filled with energy. Breath by breath, Qi Gong awakens harmony — between self and nature, body and spirit, form and flow.

Inner Smile / Taoist Energy Practices
The Inner Smile is one of the most gentle, nourishing, and trauma-informed energy meditations available. Rooted in Taoist tradition, it is based on the understanding that our internal organs are not just physiological systems — they are emotional and spiritual centers as well.

Each organ holds both emotion and wisdom. The liver stores anger and the power of transformation. The lungs carry grief and the capacity for courage. The heart pulses with joy, but also holds the remnants of sorrow and betrayal. The kidneys harbor fear and the seed of wisdom. The spleen processes worry, but also knows deep trust.

In the Inner Smile practice, the meditator gently directs a loving, radiant smile inward — organ by organ — softening tension, transmuting heavy emotions, and infusing each system with gratitude. This inner gaze is not mechanical; it is tender and sincere. Over time, the body responds — not as an object to be fixed, but as a friend finally being seen.

Often combined with the Microcosmic Orbit (a technique that circulates energy through the spine and front body), this practice restores harmony to the entire energy system. It is especially powerful for those healing chronic illness, nervous system dysregulation, or emotional trauma.

The Inner Smile teaches us that love is medicine — and the body is listening. This practice invites the soul to take up residence in the body again — not as a guest, but as a sovereign inhabitant.

Somatic and energetic meditation styles offer an essential truth: the body is sacred. The breath is sacred. The energy moving through us is sacred. Healing does not happen only in the intellect — it happens in the pulse, the gut, the spine, the subtle field. These practices bypass spiritual bypassing. They ground our awareness, soften our defenses, and reweave the inner landscape with grace.

To meditate in this way is to say to the body: *I trust you. I am listening. You are home.*

And from this sacred listening, a new flow begins — not one imposed from the outside, but arising from the deep well within. A flow that restores, regenerates, and reconnects us with the living intelligence of the body and the radiant wisdom of the soul.

Spiritual Communion & Mystical Practices

Entering the Sacred Through Union and Devotion
While many meditation forms guide us toward clarity, presence, or healing, mystical meditation reaches deeper—it is not merely about finding peace, but dissolving into the Divine. These practices speak the language of the soul: prayer, surrender, silence, ecstasy, and remembrance. They transcend method and arrive at mystery. Mystical meditation is not something you "do"—it is something you yield to. A direct, devotional, and often transformative union with the Infinite. Whether through breath or movement, chant or stillness, these practices do not just calm the mind—they open the heart. They create a threshold between the known and the eternal.

Each of the following paths comes from a distinct spiritual lineage, yet all share a common impulse: to merge with something greater, to become one with the Beloved, and to embody divinity through lived experience.

Contemplative Prayer (Christian Mysticism)
At the heart of Christian mysticism lies contemplative prayer—a meditative resting in the presence of God, beyond thought, language, or form. Unlike traditional prayer, which involves words of petition or praise, contemplative prayer is a sacred yielding. It is not about doing or achieving; it is about being with the Divine in silent communion. The practitioner sits in stillness and opens to God not as concept, but as presence.

Rooted in the desert traditions of the early Christian hermits, contemplative prayer was later shaped by great mystics such as Teresa of Ávila, John of the Cross, Julian of Norwich, and Thomas Merton. Their writings speak of inner silence, the purifying darkness of the soul, and the rapturous intimacy that can arise when one surrenders identity to the infinite.

In practice, a sacred word (like "Peace," "Abba," or "Love") may be silently repeated to center attention. But the aim is not mental control—it is consent. Consent to be transformed. To be known by Love. To be met beyond the ego, in the raw vulnerability of presence. Modern contemplative circles, such as the Centering Prayer movement led by Thomas Keating, continue to offer these ancient methods to modern seekers—particularly those longing to reconnect with Christ-consciousness while healing from religious wounds. It is a path of reverence, humility, and mystical union—where the soul does not speak, but listens.

Kabbalistic Meditation
In Jewish mysticism, known as Kabbalah, meditation is a journey into the hidden architecture of creation. It is not merely a practice—it is a revelation of the Divine blueprint encoded within the cosmos and the self. Kabbalistic meditation engages the intellect, imagination, and spirit through sacred symbols, Hebrew letters, and visualizations designed to elevate the soul.

A core structure used in Kabbalah is the Tree of Life, a map of divine emanations known as the Sephirot.

Each Sephirah represents a spiritual quality—like Wisdom (Chokhmah), Compassion (Chesed), or Beauty (Tiferet)—and by meditating on these, one refines aspects of the self and comes into greater alignment with the Divine. Other Kabbalistic techniques involve chanting sacred names of God (such as YHVH or Elohim), visualizing descending light, or using permutations of Hebrew letters to activate specific spiritual vibrations.

These practices were historically reserved for highly trained mystics, but in modern times, many teachers have opened the door to a wider audience, making these profound tools accessible without diminishing their depth. Kabbalistic meditation invites seekers into communion with the hidden layers of reality, illuminating both the light and shadow within. It is a meditative path for the mystic who longs for structure, symbolism, and a deep connection to divine order.

Sufi Whirling
In the mystical tradition of Sufism—the esoteric path of Islam—devotion becomes dance, and prayer becomes poetry in motion. Sufi whirling, or Sema, is one of the most profound embodied meditations on the planet. The whirler spins in rhythmic surrender, one hand reaching to the heavens to receive divine grace, the other extended toward the earth in offering. Through breath, music, and repetition, the practitioner enters a trance of love, dissolving into the spiral of divine remembrance.

Inspired by the teachings of the poet-mystic Rumi and practiced most famously by the Mevlevi Order, whirling is not a performance—it is a sacred act of devotion. With each turn, the ego loosens, and the heart opens wider. Accompanied by sacred music, poetry, or chants of divine names, the body becomes a living vessel for union.

Beyond whirling, Sufi meditation also includes dhikr (repetitive invocation of divine names), breathwork, and heart-focused remembrance. These practices cultivate ecstasy, longing, and deep spiritual intimacy. Sufi meditation teaches us that not all sacredness is silent—some is song, some is spin, some is tears. And through it all, the soul dances its way back to God.

Blue Rose / Magdalene Lineage Meditations
The Blue Rose tradition is a sacred feminine lineage that flows through time and space, weaving together the wisdom streams of Mary Magdalene, Mother Mary, the Essenes, the Egyptian priestesshood, and star lineages such as the Pleiadians and Sirians. These meditations awaken the body temple, especially the heart, womb, and throat centers, and call forth remembrance of one's divine essence and spiritual mission.

Blue Rose meditations often include visualizations of blue or pink rose light blooming from the heart or womb, geometric activations such as the rose spiral or vesica piscis, and sacred union journeys where the inner Divine Feminine and Masculine meet in hieros gamos. Practitioners may channel light language, receive transmissions from ascended masters, or connect with the Magdalene collective, Isis, or other sacred feminine guides.

These meditations are especially powerful for those reclaiming their voice, healing from patriarchal wounding, or awakening ancient soul contracts from lives of spiritual service. They are deeply intuitive, sensual, and soul-coded. The focus is not on transcending the body but on embodying divinity—becoming the Living Temple. The Blue Rose path is a reclamation of mystery, sovereignty, and sacred devotion. It does not ask you to follow—it asks you to remember who you are and why you came.

Shamanic Journeying
Shamanic meditation is one of the oldest spiritual technologies known to humankind. Practiced in different forms across Indigenous cultures worldwide, shamanic journeying involves entering an altered state of consciousness to access the spirit world. With the help of rhythmic drumming, breath, rattles, or ceremonial plant medicines, the practitioner "travels" into non-ordinary reality to connect with spirit allies, power animals, ancestors, and archetypal forces of nature.

There are generally three "worlds" one might journey to: the Lower World, where one may retrieve soul fragments or work with animal guides; the Upper World, where celestial beings, star wisdom, and future timelines can be accessed; and the Middle World, where energetic patterns in this realm—on land, in relationships, or within the body—can be observed and shifted.

Shamanic journeys are not guided visualizations made by the mind. They unfold organically and often carry powerful imagery, emotion, and insight. The practitioner may not remember every detail, but the energetic imprint remains. These meditations culminate in acts of integration—ritual, offering, art, or movement. Shamanic practice honors the truth that we are never alone. We walk with allies, wisdom keepers, and elemental guardians. We are part of an invisible web of life that longs to support our becoming.

Spiritual communion is not limited to saints or mystics—it is available to every soul willing to listen. Whether you whisper sacred names in silence, spiral in movement, sit beneath the stars, or feel rose petals blooming from your chest, the Divine meets you where you are. These practices do not ask for perfection. They ask for presence. They do not demand belief. They invite remembrance.

Because the greatest mystery is not that the Divine exists—but that it exists within you.

You are not reaching toward the sacred.
You are awakening to the truth that you have always been it.

Earth & Elemental Connection Meditations

Rewilding the Soul Through the Living World
Before there were temples, there were trees. Before there were sacred texts, there were rivers. Before there was doctrine, there was the Earth — pulsing with wisdom, whispering the sacred through wind, fire, water, and stone. Elemental meditation is among the most ancient and instinctual forms of spiritual practice. It asks nothing but presence. No special posture, mantra, or technique is required — only a willingness to listen. These meditations are not escapes from the world but returns to it. They bring the practitioner into intimate, embodied dialogue with life itself — with the natural forces that mirror our internal patterns and guide us back to balance.

The five classical elements — Earth, Water, Fire, Air, and Ether — are more than poetic archetypes. They are living energies, resonant blueprints that exist both within us and throughout the natural world. To meditate with them is to return to wholeness, to feel again our place within the web of life. These practices reconnect the human and the holy, inviting us to remember that we are not separate from the Earth but made of her.

Fire Meditation (Candle Gazing / Agni Drishti)
Fire meditations are initiatory by nature. Fire is the element of transformation, purification, and sacred will. It burns away illusion and awakens clarity. A foundational practice is candle gazing — known as Trataka or Agni Drishti in yogic traditions — where a

single flame becomes the anchor of attention. Sitting in darkness with a candle placed at eye level, the practitioner holds a soft gaze on the flame without blinking, and then closes the eyes to witness the afterimage in the third eye space. This simple act sharpens concentration, activates inner sight, and opens pathways of insight and illumination. Fire meditations can also be more expansive — envisioning flames moving through the spine to awaken dormant energy, or sitting in ritual with a ceremonial fire, releasing grief, anger, or outdated identities into the flame's alchemical embrace. Fire is the sacred destroyer and the holy spark. It teaches us how to transmute, how to lead, and how to rise — again and again — from our own ashes.

Water Meditation (Flow, Emotion, Ritual Bathing)
Water meditations bring us into the realm of feeling, intuition, and memory. Water holds emotion, depth, and the story of everything it has ever touched. When we sit beside a river or ocean, bathe in sacred waters, or visualize cleansing streams moving through the body, we enter the current of surrender. Water softens rigidity and teaches us to move with, rather than against, life's flow. Ritual bathing, especially with herbs, salts, or oils, transforms ordinary self-care into sacred ceremony — a reconsecration of the body and spirit. These meditations help release grief, dissolve emotional stagnation, and reconnect with the inner child or dreamtime wisdom. Working with the Moon's tides adds an additional layer — aligning with waxing and waning cycles for intention, release, and renewal. Water invites us to feel, to trust, and to remember that healing is not linear, but tidal.

Earth Meditation (Rooting, Grounding, Stone Connection)

Earth meditations are grounding, centering, and deeply restorative. In a world that pulls us into overstimulation and fragmentation, Earth calls us back to slowness, to solidity, to home. Meditating directly on the ground — lying on the soil, sitting at the base of a tree, or standing barefoot in the grass — initiates a return to presence. Visualizing roots descending from the body into the earth helps restore the energetic boundary and reinforce the body's container. Holding stones, sitting with sacred land, or simply breathing in rhythm with the Earth's pulse can calm the nervous system and provide anchorage during emotional or spiritual upheaval. Earth meditations often feel like a conversation with the ancestors or a prayer into the bones. They are especially supportive for those doing deep trauma healing or energy work, as they offer containment, regulation, and nourishment that transcends words.

Air Meditation (Breath, Wind, Feather Work)

Air meditations awaken lightness, clarity, and movement. Air is the breath — the invisible spirit that animates all things. To meditate with air is to remember that the sacred is already moving through you, breath by breath. Practices may include intentional breathwork, such as box breathing, alternate nostril breathing, or simply focusing on extended exhalation to calm the system. Others may stand or sit in the wind, allowing it to cleanse the auric field and carry away stagnant energy. Imagery of feathers, wings, or invisible currents can be powerful in helping lift emotional weight and reconnect with creative inspiration. In many traditions, breath is synonymous with spirit — called prana, pneuma, or ruach — and air becomes the bridge between body and soul, thought and presence, silence and voice. In air meditations, the breath becomes the prayer, and each exhale becomes the release.

Ether Meditation (Akasha, Cosmic Silence)
Ether — also called Akasha or space — is the subtlest of the elements and the most expansive. It is not seen, but it contains everything. It is the silence beneath sound, the stillness behind movement, the field in which all other elements arise and dissolve. Ether meditations often unfold in silence, guiding the practitioner beyond identity and form, into pure presence. They may include accessing the Akashic field, receiving impressions from the soul's journey across time and space, or visualizing the self dissolving into luminous light or infinite void. These meditations open the gateway to non-dual awareness, multidimensional perception, and cosmic communion. Ether holds the memory of the stars within our cells, reminding us that spaciousness is not emptiness, but the pure potential of divine creation.

Plant Spirit and Tree Connection Meditations
In communion with plants and trees, meditation becomes deeply relational. Trees are not passive scenery — they are elders, timekeepers, and energetic allies. Sitting with your spine against a tree, you may begin to feel its heartbeat, its breath moving with yours. Tree meditation invites a deep listening, a return to verticality, and an attunement to grounded

wisdom. Similarly, working with specific plant spirits — whether through visualization, guided journey, or breathwork — allows the practitioner to receive guidance, healing, and energetic codes from the green world. Using sacred herbs, essential oils, or flower essences before meditation can amplify sensitivity and deepen this connection. These meditations cultivate reciprocity and ecological intimacy — a remembrance that we are part of nature, not separate from it.

Sound of the Elements / Drumming / Natural Rhythms
The Earth speaks not only through form, but through rhythm. Sound-based elemental meditation activates primal memory and re-patterns the nervous system. Drumming, rattling, chanting, or listening to natural soundscapes — waves, wind, crackling fire, birdsong — brings the body into coherence with the Earth's own frequency. Sound bypasses the thinking mind and touches something ancient in the cells. It evokes heartbeat, thunder, rain, and creation itself. When sound is woven with intention — calling in the directions, ancestors, or elemental guardians — it becomes a vibrational offering and a sacred conversation.

Elemental meditation is not a technique — it is a relationship. It is a way of returning to the wisdom that has always been available, encoded in the wind, held in the stone, dancing in the flame. To meditate with the elements is to remember that we are not above or beyond the Earth, but of her. That every breath, every heartbeat, every tear is already part of a larger rhythm — the one song of life.

You do not need to seek the sacred in far-off realms. It is beneath your feet, in your lungs, on your skin. The Earth is not waiting for you to ascend — she is inviting you to return. And when you do, she will remember you. Because you are her, and she is you.

Visual, Sacred Geometry & Fractal-Based Meditations

Awakening the Inner Eye Through Pattern, Light, and Code

Not all meditations guide us into silence or stillness. Some open the inner eye — not through imagination alone, but through frequency, shape, and cosmic design. Visual and geometry-based meditations offer an entrance into the architecture of the soul. These practices use sacred patterns, color, light, and energetic codes to recalibrate the human energy field and activate multidimensional awareness.

Sacred geometry is the blueprint of creation — the divine language written into the stars, seashells, DNA strands, and galaxies. These forms carry universal harmonics. When we meditate with them, we don't merely observe their beauty — we entrain with their intelligence. The patterns become portals, initiating alignment, remembrance, and awakening.

These practices engage the third eye, pineal gland, and intuitive faculties. They support the clearing of mental clutter and the download of higher guidance. They awaken resonance within the aura and light body — transforming meditation into a sacred act of visual communion with the cosmos.

Mandala Gazing

Mandalas are sacred visual forms that symbolize wholeness, unity, and the cyclical nature of existence. Found in Hindu, Buddhist, Indigenous, and Jungian traditions, they serve as both a mirror of the inner world and a map toward integration. Mandala gazing is the meditative practice of visually focusing on a mandala, often painted or drawn, and allowing its symmetrical form to guide consciousness inward. Over time, thoughts soften, and the spiral geometry pulls awareness into the still point — the center of the self.

Creating mandalas can also be a form of meditation. Whether drawn, painted, or constructed with natural materials, the process becomes a ritual that reveals internal patterns and initiates energetic balance. Mandalas speak to the soul in symbols, awakening archetypes and restoring coherence in the mind and field. They are visual mantras — carriers of presence, intention, and healing.

Sacred Geometry: Merkaba, Flower of Life, and Metatron's Cube

Sacred geometry encompasses timeless energetic patterns found in all life. These symbols are not just visual — they are vibrational technologies that carry the intelligence of creation. The Merkaba, for example, is a three-dimensional star tetrahedron — two interlocking pyramids spinning in opposite directions — representing the integration of divine masculine and feminine, spirit and matter. It is the light body vehicle used for protection, multidimensional travel, and spiritual ascension.

The Flower of Life, composed of multiple interlocking circles, is a powerful symbol of creation and the interconnectedness of all things. It holds within it the patterns of DNA, musical harmonics, and planetary cycles. Meditating with the Flower of Life attunes us to sacred order and cosmic remembrance. Another potent form is Metatron's Cube, which contains the five Platonic solids and is used to clear, align, and transmit divine intelligence. Many lightworkers use Metatron's Cube as a visual seal for energetic protection or as a conduit for high-frequency channeling.

These forms may be visualized, traced with the hands, built energetically around the aura, or gazed upon during meditation. When engaged consciously, they act as tuning forks for the soul — initiating coherence between the body, field, and higher realms.

Fractal Visualizations and Infinite Pattern Awareness

Fractals are infinite patterns that repeat at different scales. They are seen in nature — in ferns, trees, coastlines, snowflakes — and in cosmic design. They represent the principle of "as above, so below." In meditation, visualizing fractals can create a powerful sense of pattern recognition and expansion beyond time. The practitioner might visualize spirals, kaleidoscopic forms, or recursive geometry unfolding infinitely inward or outward.

Fractal meditations can induce deep trance states, especially for neurodivergent or highly visual individuals, offering a calming yet dynamic focus for the mind. They awaken the intuitive brain, stimulate the pineal gland, and open the pathways to insight, integration, and multidimensional understanding. These visual loops are not random — they are echoes of the divine design pulsing through all creation.

Color-Coded Light Meditations: Chakras, Rays, and Auras

Color is vibration made visible. When we meditate with color, we are not just seeing light — we are feeling frequency. Color-coded meditations use specific hues to cleanse, activate, and align the chakras, aura, and energy field. A red light at the root may ground and restore vitality, while a violet flame in the crown may initiate transmutation and ascension. These meditations can be used to rebalance emotions, activate chakra centers, or attune to specific spiritual rays.

Beyond chakra work, some lightworkers engage with the Seven Sacred Rays or with color-coded angelic or cosmic frequencies, each associated with a specific virtue, guide, or evolutionary frequency. You might visualize beams of green healing light, blue rays of protection and truth, or golden frequencies of divine will. Color-coded light can also be used to repair the auric field, clear energy cords, or reestablish energetic boundaries.

These meditations are especially useful for healers, empaths, and intuitive practitioners seeking to maintain energetic hygiene or guide clients into energetic clarity. They serve as both clearing tools and activation templates, providing subtle recalibration through vibrational resonance.

Light Language and Geometric Code Activation
Light language is the soul's multidimensional voice — a vibrational form of communication that bypasses the rational mind and speaks directly to the heart, DNA, and light body. It may come through as spoken sounds, song, written symbols, hand movements, or even geometry streaming in the inner eye. When used in meditation, light language serves as a carrier wave — transmitting healing, activation, and higher intelligence.

Geometric codes may be received visually in meditation or consciously drawn or invoked. These codes often appear as intricate sigils, crystalline grids, or star maps. Practitioners may call in light language or codes for specific purposes — to open the heart, unlock ancestral memory, clear the throat, or activate soul gifts. Some journey into the Akashic field or galactic dimensions through these codes, receiving downloads that awaken long-dormant frequencies.

Light language meditation may involve speaking aloud, tracing symbols over the body, toning into chakras, or simply receiving codes in silence. The process is deeply intuitive, sacred, and often unique to the soul's lineage and mission. It reconnects the practitioner with their cosmic origin, weaving soul strands back into wholeness.

Visual and geometric meditations awaken the inner eye and recode the light body. They activate memory not only of who we are, but of the greater structures we are a part of — the galaxies, the grids, the sacred blueprints of existence. These meditations speak not in words, but in color, symbol, and sound. They are mirrors and keys — sacred technologies that support ascension, embodiment, and energetic sovereignty.

To meditate in this way is to step into the role of creator, visionary, and frequency holder.
You do not just see the pattern —
You *become* the pattern.
You *remember* the geometry you were born from.
And you begin to live as the living light you are.

Galactic & Ascension-Based Meditations

Awakening the Star Within and Remembering the Mission

Galactic and ascension-based meditations guide us into the realm of multidimensional consciousness. These practices do not separate us from our human experience; they enhance it. They help us recall that we are not just physical beings having spiritual experiences, but spiritual and galactic beings having a deeply sacred human journey. These meditations activate soul-level remembrance, energetic upgrades, and planetary service. They reconnect us with our star lineages, upgrade our light body systems, and remind us of the cosmic mission we came here to fulfill.

DNA and Light Code Activation

DNA and light code activations are meditative journeys designed to awaken dormant aspects of our energetic and spiritual blueprint. While mainstream science has long referred to so-called "junk DNA," spiritual traditions and starseed teachings view this unused potential as the storage site of ancient wisdom, spiritual gifts, and multidimensional abilities. In these meditations, the practitioner consciously works with strands of quantum DNA — energetic filaments that hold information from soul lineages, past lives, and interdimensional incarnations.

During a light code activation, one may receive or visualize codes in the form of symbols, sacred geometry, light language, or tones. These codes often appear as floating glyphs, streaming light, or crystalline downloads that enter the spine, heart, or crown. Some activations happen spontaneously during meditation, while others are intentionally guided with sound, breath, or channeling. Light language — whether spoken, sung, or written — often acts as a carrier for these frequencies.

These meditations help repair distortions, reactivate spiritual memory, and recalibrate the nervous system to hold higher frequencies. They often result in emotional release, visions, or physical sensations as energy reorganizes. The purpose is not to become more than human, but to remember the fullness of our soul design — to embody more of who we truly are.

Starseed Lineage Meditation (Pleiadian, Arcturian, Lyran, etc.)

Starseed lineage meditations connect practitioners with their soul's galactic origins. A starseed is a soul whose journey includes lifetimes in other star systems or dimensions, often holding memory of service, healing, or guidance on Earth. These meditations allow the practitioner to reunite with their star family, often in the form of Pleiadian, Arcturian, Sirian, Lyran, Andromedan, or other high-frequency collectives.

During a starseed meditation, the practitioner may travel in consciousness to a starship, a crystalline temple, or a luminous galactic council chamber. Encounters often include telepathic messages, energy downloads, or emotional resonance that confirms the deep familiarity of the connection. Some receive missions, upgrades, or healing. Others simply feel the deep comfort of being seen and remembered by beings who operate from unconditional love and unity consciousness.

These meditations help us reconnect with lost aspects of identity, release the trauma of Earth density, and receive guidance for our current life path. While each star lineage holds a unique frequency — such as Pleiadian heart-wisdom, Arcturian technology and energy healing, or Lyran sovereignty and creation codes — all serve the collective awakening of Earth and the liberation of the human soul. Through this work, practitioners reclaim their multidimensional essence and activate their roles as gridworkers, healers, and frequency holders.

Higher Self Integration and Council Meeting
Higher Self integration meditations focus on building an active relationship with the most evolved and divine aspect of one's own consciousness. The Higher Self is not a guide or deity external to us — it is the luminous, unconditionally loving presence that exists beyond ego, trauma, or illusion. This part of us holds our soul's plan, timeless wisdom, and the energetic blueprint of our most aligned path.

In meditation, this integration may begin with a simple invocation or visualization — meeting your Higher Self in a light chamber, a sacred garden, or a temple space. Often, this presence appears as a version of yourself — radiant, whole, and deeply familiar. Communication may occur through telepathy, light codes, touch, or direct knowing. The practitioner may ask for guidance, receive healing, or merge with this aspect in order to embody its frequency more fully.

Some Higher Self meditations also include meetings with a soul council or galactic council — groups of guides, ancestors, or multidimensional beings who support the soul's evolution. These councils often offer insight into the soul's purpose, karmic patterns, and future timelines. These meditations create a framework for trust, empowerment, and aligned decision-making in daily life. As the practitioner integrates with the Higher Self, they begin to live from their divine intelligence — becoming the bridge between heaven and earth.

Planetary Grid Meditations and Collective Healing
Planetary grid meditations expand consciousness beyond personal healing and into collective service. These practices involve connecting with Gaia's crystalline and energetic grid — the vast web of energy lines, vortexes, and ley lines that hold Earth's energetic architecture. Many ancient sacred sites — such as the pyramids of Egypt, Stonehenge, Machu Picchu, and Uluru — are key points within this grid.

Lightworkers and gridkeepers often feel called to activate or anchor light at these sites, both physically and energetically.

In planetary grid work meditation, the practitioner may visualize themselves as a conduit of light, anchoring energy from Source or the galactic center down through the body and into the Earth. Light can be directed into wounded areas of the planet, places of violence or imbalance, or to amplify harmony in sites of ancient power. Practitioners often work during celestial alignments — such as solstices, equinoxes, eclipses, or full moons — when the Earth's field is more responsive and open to quantum input.

These meditations may also include global healing visualizations — sending waves of peace, unity, or truth across timelines, populations, or collective trauma fields. The intention is never to "fix," but to harmonize, support, and co-create with the Earth's consciousness. This work helps stabilize ascension energies, reduce energetic chaos, and weave humanity into greater resonance with Gaia's evolution.

Grid meditations also assist in anchoring light codes from higher dimensions into the physical plane. As practitioners remember their role in planetary service, these meditations become acts of deep spiritual devotion and sacred responsibility. The Earth responds when we show up in this way — not as saviors, but as partners in her birthing process.

These galactic and ascension-based practices are for those who remember there is more. More than the body. More than the mind. More than this lifetime. They speak to the part of you that has always been watching, waiting, and listening for the moment of activation — the moment you stop playing small and step into your soul's assignment. Through these meditations, we don't leave Earth — we help lift it. We don't bypass humanity — we infuse it with divinity. We become the bridge, the beacon, the vessel through which higher light can move.

To meditate in this way is to come home to your most radiant self.
Not as something to reach for —
But as something you've always been.

Therapeutic & Trauma-Informed Practices

Safety as the Foundation of Healing
While meditation is often praised for its calming effects, it is important to recognize that traditional meditation styles can sometimes be dysregulating or even re-traumatizing for individuals with complex trauma or nervous system sensitivity. Therapeutic and trauma-informed meditation practices are specifically designed to meet the body where it is — honoring internal signals, inviting consent-based awareness, and fostering a sense of safety rather than pushing toward transcendence. These practices support emotional regulation, inner resourcing, and embodied presence. They are particularly valuable for those navigating PTSD, C-PTSD, chronic illness, neurodivergence, or developmental trauma.

Safe Space Visualizations
Safe space visualizations are foundational in trauma-informed meditation and hypnotherapy. In these meditations, the practitioner is guided to create an inner sanctuary — a space that feels calm, nourishing, and free from harm. This imagined space may be a meadow, temple, room, forest, or other personalized setting that evokes a sense of comfort, agency, and grounding. Within this visualization, one can invite inner allies, protective guides, or soothing sensory elements like soft light, warmth, gentle textures, or familiar sounds.

These visualizations are especially effective at the beginning of a healing journey, during flashback recovery, or when anchoring the nervous system after emotional processing. They allow the subconscious mind to associate inner exploration with calm and safety, which is essential for trauma integration. Over time, this internal sanctuary becomes a go-to resource — a remembered place the nervous system can return to during moments of distress or overwhelm.

Parts Work and Inner Dialogue Meditation
Inspired by modalities like Internal Family Systems (IFS), Voice Dialogue, and Gestalt, parts work meditations involve entering into conversation with distinct inner voices or sub-personalities that make up the psyche. Trauma often leads to the fragmentation of self — creating "parts" that hold specific roles such as protector, wounded child, inner critic, rebel, or pleaser. Through meditation, one can meet these parts with curiosity and compassion, allowing them to speak, express, and be witnessed without judgment.

In this inner dialogue, the meditator may invite a part to step forward, listen to its concerns or needs, and explore its origin story. Often, what initially presents as sabotage or fear is revealed to be a younger version of the self simply trying to stay safe. By acknowledging and integrating these parts, the practitioner builds internal trust and begins to reweave the fragmented aspects of their psyche into a coherent, compassionate whole.

This style of meditation is especially powerful for survivors of trauma, attachment wounds, and inner conflict. It supports emotional regulation, reparenting, and the deep restoration of inner unity.

Somatic Sensing and Felt Sense Awareness
Somatic and felt sense meditations draw awareness into the body's subtle language — the quiet signals that arise before words or emotion. Developed through practices like Somatic Experiencing, Focusing (Gendlin), and body-based mindfulness, these meditations train the practitioner to observe and be with bodily sensations without trying to fix, judge, or escape them. A tightening in the chest, a flutter in the stomach, a pressure behind the eyes — these are not just physical reactions; they are information, communication, memory.

The practitioner may be guided to notice sensations with descriptive awareness (e.g., warm, pulsing, tingling, hollow) and to stay with them gently, following the subtle shifts that arise. This process allows trapped energy, emotion, or memory to slowly unravel. It also helps rebuild interoception — the body's ability to feel and respond to internal cues — which is often disrupted in trauma.

Somatic meditations reconnect us with the wisdom of the body and create the conditions for authentic healing. Rather than leaving the body to access spirit, this practice reclaims the body *as* spirit — a living temple of sensation, memory, and soul.

Heart Coherence and Nervous System Balancing
Heart coherence meditation is a scientifically validated technique that brings the brain, heart, and nervous system into harmonic alignment. Developed in part by the HeartMath Institute, this practice involves slowing the breath, focusing attention on the heart, and cultivating elevated emotional states such as gratitude, compassion, and peace. As heart rhythm variability stabilizes, the nervous system shifts out of fight-or-flight and into parasympathetic restoration.

In meditation, the practitioner might place their hand on the heart, breathe in a slow rhythm (e.g., five seconds in, five seconds out), and visualize the breath moving in and out of the heart space. From there, they can intentionally generate a feeling of appreciation or warmth, allowing it to expand through the body.

This method is powerful for calming anxiety, lowering cortisol, and improving emotional resilience. It can be paired with affirmations, intention-setting, or energy work to enhance its impact. For trauma survivors, it becomes a gentle and empowering way to self-regulate without bypassing or suppressing emotion. When practiced regularly, heart coherence supports a rewiring of the nervous system toward safety, connection, and emotional spaciousness.

Together, these trauma-informed and therapeutic meditations offer a different model of healing — one rooted in listening, presence, and permission. They do not force the practitioner into stillness, silence, or transcendence. Instead, they hold space for real-time integration, honoring the body's intelligence and pacing. For those who have long felt unsafe in their own minds or bodies, these practices become a pathway home — not to an idealized version of self, but to the self as it is, worthy of love, wholeness, and breath.

These meditations are not just spiritual. They are biological, emotional, ancestral, and relational. They are the foundation upon which all deeper work can rest. Because without safety, there is no healing. And without embodiment, there is no liberation.

Part III: Creating & Facilitating Meditations

Creating Meditations for Personal Practice

Reclaiming the Sacred Within
Meditation does not have to be sourced from ancient texts, prestigious teachers, or spiritual lineages — it can rise organically from within you. While many people begin with pre-recorded meditations or traditional techniques, there is a moment in every seeker's journey when they are invited to turn inward and craft their own practice. This chapter is devoted to that moment — when the external map becomes an internal compass, and you begin listening to the whisper of your own soul.

To create your own meditation practice is to acknowledge yourself as a source of wisdom. It is to trust that your body, your spirit, and your energy field already know what you need — and that meditation is not about "getting it right," but about entering into honest, consistent relationship with yourself. Your practice does not need to be elaborate. It needs to be real. The following guiding principles can support you in developing a personal meditation practice that is sustainable, sacred, and deeply aligned with your life's rhythms.

Developing a Sacred Space
Creating a physical space for your meditation practice helps signal to your mind and body that you are entering sacred time. This space doesn't need to be large or ornate — it only needs to feel safe, intentional, and energetically clear. You might designate a corner of a room, a cushion by a window,

or an altar with meaningful objects such as candles, crystals, feathers, plants, or photographs.

Energetically cleanse the space regularly using sound, smoke (such as sage, palo santo, or mugwort), water, or light visualizations. Keep the area free of clutter and electronics when possible. This becomes your inner temple — a place where the veil between worlds thins, and you are invited to come as you are. Over time, the energetic imprint of your consistent practice will build, creating a field of support that makes entering meditative states more effortless.

Listening to Your Inner Voice
While it's valuable to learn from external guidance, your most potent meditation teacher will always be your own inner voice. You might begin your practice by placing one hand on your heart and the other on your belly, simply asking: *What do I need today?* Trust whatever image, phrase, body sensation, or instinct arises. That is your doorway.

Some days you may need silence. Other days, movement. Sometimes breath, or prayer, or visualization. Meditation is not a performance. It is a conversation — and the first step in that conversation is listening. Journaling before or after your practice can help capture the insights that emerge, and over time, patterns will reveal themselves. You'll begin to sense when your body is asking for grounding, when your energy wants expansion, and when your heart simply wants to be witnessed.

Aligning with Daily, Lunar, or Seasonal Rhythms
Your personal meditation practice can be greatly enhanced by syncing with the natural rhythms that already shape your life. Just as the Earth moves through seasons, your inner world flows through cycles of birth, growth, release, and rest. Aligning your practice with these rhythms brings deeper resonance and harmony to your inner work.

Daily rhythms: Consider the energetic tone of different times of day. Morning meditations may focus on intention setting, energizing breathwork, or solar alignment. Evening meditations might center on reflection, clearing, or dream incubation. Let your daily energy levels guide the structure and purpose of your practice.

Lunar rhythms: The moon's cycles offer profound meditative portals. The new moon is ideal for planting intentions and entering the void. The full moon amplifies emotional clarity, manifestation, and illumination. Waning phases support release and forgiveness, while waxing phases foster growth and momentum. Create rituals or guided journeys that correspond to each phase, using lunar energy as an ally in your spiritual development.

Seasonal rhythms: Earth's turning seasons affect both the external landscape and your internal energetic flow. Spring calls for awakening and emergence. Summer invites embodiment and creativity. Autumn teaches surrender and integration. Winter holds space for stillness, rest, and rebirth. Tuning into the themes of each season can inform the tone of your practice — from the imagery you use to the breath patterns you follow.

Your practice does not need to be fixed or formulaic. It can evolve with you — changing with your mood, your needs, your environment, and your becoming. Meditation, in its truest form, is a dynamic relationship between you and the sacred. It is a homecoming. A recalibration. A remembering.

There are no rules in this remembering — only invitations.
To pause.
To feel.
To follow the thread of aliveness.
To meet yourself, again and again, in the sacred breath between moments.

Creating and Leading Meditations for Clients & Groups

Facilitating Sacred Transformation Through Conscious Presence
This chapter is the heart of this book — a living transmission for those called to lead others into sacred space. Whether you are a therapist, coach, healer, energy worker, yoga teacher, or simply a seeker who wishes to hold space for others, learning how to create and facilitate meditations is an art form that blends intuition, structure, presence, trauma sensitivity, and energetic mastery.

When someone enters your space — whether one-on-one or in a group — they are opening a vulnerable doorway. They are placing their trust in your presence. Your ability to guide them through the inner terrain of emotion, memory, energy, and vision is not about reciting words — it is about how you hold space, how you transmit safety, and how you read the field. This chapter is devoted to helping you cultivate those capacities with integrity, confidence, and sacred attunement.

Holding Energetic Space
Before you ever speak a word, the energetic space you hold is already shaping the container. Holding space is not about being perfect or enlightened — it is about being grounded, clear, present, and attuned to what is alive in the room (seen and unseen). Your nervous system sets the tone. Your inner alignment becomes the resonance others entrain to. This is

especially important in meditation and hypnosis, where participants drop into theta states and become more open, suggestible, and energetically permeable.

To hold energetic space, begin by grounding yourself fully before beginning. Feel your feet, your breath, your center. Clear your own energy using breath, intention, or visualization. Set the intention for the session or group. Call in your highest self, guides, or the divine as you define it. Ask to be a clear, humble, and safe channel. Protect and cleanse the space using sound, smoke, water, salt, or visualization. You may wish to create a light field or protective sphere around the space or group.

Throughout the session, maintain energetic awareness. Stay attuned to shifts in the field — someone's breath changing, a sudden emotional wave, or intuitive impressions. Anchor the container. You are the lighthouse. Others may journey into deep places, but your job is to stay centered, loving, and unshaken, holding the frequency. Energetic spaceholding becomes stronger the more you practice and clear your own inner distortions. Your presence is the medicine. Your neutrality is the sanctuary.

Voice, Tone, and Language
Your voice is not just a tool — it is an instrument of alchemy. The tone, pace, and rhythm of your speech can guide someone from beta brainwaves to theta or delta. Your language becomes the landscape they journey through. This is especially important when working with neurodivergent, highly sensitive, or

trauma-affected individuals, for whom tone and sensory processing are amplified.

Speak slowly and intentionally, leaving space between phrases. Use a soft, grounded tone and avoid overly theatrical or overly detached delivery. Let your voice drop into your body — speak from the heart, not just the head. Practice modulating volume and inflection to maintain engagement without overstimulation.

Use present-tense, invitational language. For example: "You may begin to notice..." or "Allow yourself to feel..." rather than "You are now..." Avoid commanding or assumptive language. Let participants have agency. Use sensory-rich descriptions to guide visualization (sight, sound, texture, scent). Affirm safety and choice throughout: "Only as much as feels comfortable," "You are always in control," "You may return to the breath at any time."

Avoid triggering language unless you are specifically trained in trauma processing. Refrain from "fixing," diagnosing, or assuming what the client is feeling. The goal is not to direct their experience but to guide them to their own.

Group Dynamics, Trauma Awareness & Consent
Leading groups adds complexity — and power. The group field amplifies healing, but also requires strong boundaries, attunement, and trauma-informed facilitation. Every group holds a mix of nervous systems, triggers, attachment styles, spiritual beliefs, and personal histories. Your job is to create a

container where everyone feels safe, seen, and sovereign.

Establish consent up front. Explain what kind of meditation you'll be doing, what participants can expect, and what their options are. Invite questions. Normalize a range of experiences. Let people know it's okay to feel emotional, numb, distracted, or activated. There is no "wrong" experience. Offer options. Let participants know they can lie down or sit, keep eyes open or closed, journal instead of meditating — adapt to their needs.

Create safety agreements. Especially in therapeutic or spiritual spaces, co-create agreements such as confidentiality, mutual respect, and no cross-talk during shares. Honor cultural, neurodivergent, and spiritual diversity. Avoid language or symbolism that could alienate or retraumatize participants. Be open to feedback. Debrief gently. After meditation, guide a grounding practice. Offer space for integration — either through sharing, journaling, or quiet reflection. Don't rush people back into the external world.

As a facilitator, you must become fluent in the language of subtle cues. Pay attention to body language such as tense shoulders, shifting posture, or fidgeting. Notice breath patterns like rapid breathing, breath holding, or sighing. Be aware of emotional cues such as tears, silence, laughter, or dissociation.

Have tools ready for grounding or emotional support. This could include breathwork, somatic resourcing, or even pausing the session if necessary.

Leading meditation is sacred. You are guiding others into altered states of consciousness. Do not take this lightly. Practice humility. Do your own work. Stay within your scope of practice. If you're not trained in trauma processing, avoid leading regressions or deep emotional excavation. Refer out when needed. And always, always prioritize consent and integration.

Facilitating meditation is not about performance. It's not about knowing the right words or crafting a perfect script. It is about how you show up. Your presence. Your frequency. Your love.

You are not here to fix people. You are here to hold a mirror to their own divinity. You are here to open a doorway — and trust that their soul will walk through it in perfect timing.

Lead from your heart. Anchor in your body. Listen to the unseen. And trust that every time you guide another into stillness, into story, or into light — you are midwifing something sacred back into the world.

You are not just a facilitator. You are a sacred spaceholder. And that, beloved, is holy work.

Designing General vs. Custom Meditations

Balancing Structure, Soul, and the Sacred Specific
Creating meditation is both an art and a science — a practice that requires both structure and sensitivity, both thematic clarity and intuitive responsiveness. Whether you're designing a meditation to serve the general public or crafting a journey for a specific individual, it's essential to understand the difference in approach, purpose, and energetic design. In this chapter, we explore how to build meditations that are universally supportive or uniquely tailored, and how to let the soul of a meditation reveal itself through intention, archetype, and resonance.

Thematic Structures (e.g., Calm, Focus, Healing)
General meditations are designed to address universal human experiences — stress, overwhelm, anxiety, lack of focus, insomnia, grief, creativity blocks, or the desire for spiritual connection. These meditations usually follow a familiar arc or structure: grounding and arrival, breath awareness, the main thematic experience (such as body relaxation, heart opening, or visualization), and a gentle return.

Themes provide a backbone. When designing general meditations, consider what state you want the listener to enter or cultivate. Is it calm? Confidence? Clarity? Then reverse engineer the elements of the meditation — breath pacing, imagery, tone, affirmations — to lead them there. For instance, a meditation for calm may include deep belly breathing, oceanic imagery, and soft descending tones. A focus meditation may include alert postures, candle gazing, breath retention, and sharp mental imagery (like visualizing light through a laser lens).

General meditations are best used in group settings, online offerings, apps, and for those who may be new to inner work. They cast a wide net and are excellent tools for regulation, entry into practice, and consistency. They are also useful for practitioners who want a repeatable format or are working with groups where individual needs can't be directly addressed. However, they must still be intentional and energetically coherent — just because they are general doesn't mean they are generic.

Personalized Meditations for Specific Client Needs
Custom meditations, by contrast, are living soul maps — designed to meet one unique person exactly where they are. These meditations are tailored to their emotional landscape, energetic blueprint, trauma history, nervous system regulation patterns, soul contracts, and intentions for growth. Creating personalized meditations requires deep listening, intuitive perception, and often a pre-session dialogue or intake process.

You might ask the client: What are you struggling with right now? What do you long for? What's showing up in your body, your dreams, your emotions? What is your nervous system asking for — stimulation, soothing, integration, expression? These questions shape the medicine.

A personalized meditation may include:

- Naming and validating the client's lived experience
- Guided imagery that reflects symbols from their own inner world
- Specific chakra or energy field work based on intuitive or clinical assessment
- Soul retrieval, inner child healing, ancestral clearing, or reparenting components
- Affirmations or phrases drawn from the client's own voice

These meditations become mirrors — helping clients witness themselves with compassion, access subconscious material safely, and rehearse new beliefs or possibilities in an embodied way. Custom meditations are especially powerful for trauma survivors, neurodivergent clients, spiritual seekers in transition, and those navigating grief, identity shifts, or spiritual emergence.

Personalized journeys require ethical presence. Do not insert your own agenda or projections. Allow the imagery, pacing, and tone to match the nervous system and soul-state of the client. Be willing to adjust in real time. And always offer follow-up space for integration.

Working with Archetypes, Intentions, and Soul Codes

Whether general or personalized, the most powerful meditations are encoded with archetypal and energetic intelligence. Archetypes are universal energies — patterns of consciousness such as the Inner Child, the Warrior, the Sage, the Mother, the Shadow. When we invite archetypes into meditation, we give form to the formless. We help the subconscious speak in a language it understands.

For example, instead of saying "you feel confident," you might guide the client to meet their Inner Queen or Warrior, who carries their confidence and embodied boundaries. Instead of talking about clarity, you may invite them into a crystal temple or to gaze into a sacred mirror. These symbols bypass logic and speak directly to the soul.

Intentions act as energetic anchors. Every meditation should begin with a clear intention, whether spoken aloud or internally held. This might be as simple as "I return to my breath" or as expansive as "I awaken my divine remembrance." Intentions calibrate the field. They magnetize synchronicities. They inform the intelligence of the journey.

Soul codes refer to vibrational keys — often carried through voice, imagery, light language, or geometry — that activate latent potentials in the listener. These are often channeled or intuitively transmitted and are unique to the facilitator's frequency. When included skillfully, soul codes turn a meditation from a relaxation exercise into a multidimensional activation.

Whether you are writing a meditation for a thousand listeners or one sacred soul, what matters most is your presence. Let the meditation write itself through you. Listen to the field. Trust the metaphors. Follow the breath. And always — always — return to love as the guiding frequency.

Meditation design is not about formula. It is about frequency. And when your frequency is aligned with truth, what you create will ripple far beyond words.

Part IV: Integration & Embodiment

The Meditation Path as a Way of Life

Becoming the Practice You Seek
Meditation does not end when the music fades or when the timer goes off. It is not confined to cushions, candles, or carefully curated spaces. While these sacred rituals are beautiful and powerful, they are only doorways — not destinations. The true essence of meditation is how we meet life itself. How we respond in the in-between moments. How we breathe when no one is watching. How we return to presence again and again, even in chaos.

Everyday Presence
To live the meditation path is to live in presence. It is to choose awareness — in your thoughts, your emotions, your interactions, and your actions. You begin to notice your inner world not just during practice, but while making tea, folding laundry, or driving your child to school. Presence is not about perfection or constant bliss. It is about relationship — with breath, with body, with truth. In the smallest moments, we are offered the opportunity to slow down, to witness, to soften.

This doesn't require a set script or a sacred soundtrack. It requires attention. When we greet the moment fully — whether joyful, painful, or mundane — we become the witness and the participant. We are meditating in motion. Every step, every blink, every breath becomes sacred. It is not a performance, but a deepening into what is real. Meditation becomes the ground of our being, not just an escape from it.

Meditation Beyond the Cushion
One of the great myths of spiritual practice is that it must be separate from "ordinary life." But what if the most ordinary acts — sweeping the floor, chopping vegetables, or tending a crying baby — are not distractions from the path, but the path itself?

Meditation beyond the cushion invites us to bring sacred awareness into daily life. You don't need an hour of silence. You need a moment of intention. Five conscious breaths before answering the phone. A pause before you react. A silent blessing over your food. A grounding breath between clients. These tiny acts recalibrate the nervous system and attune your energy field. They keep you anchored. Embodied. Aligned.

Even in grief, rage, or confusion — presence is possible. Meditation teaches us that we don't have to fix every feeling or understand every thought. We just need to sit with them. To breathe with them. To honor the wave without becoming it.

Living as the Embodied Temple
Eventually, the line between the practitioner and the practice dissolves. You are not just someone who *does* meditation. You become the meditation. You become the transmission. Your life becomes the altar.

This is the essence of the Embodied Temple — to walk through the world as a living sanctuary. To recognize that your body is holy, your emotions are sacred currents, your voice is a bell of truth, and your presence is a healing force. Every interaction becomes an offering. Every breath a prayer.

Living this way is not always easy. It asks you to confront your shadows, regulate your nervous system, take accountability, and rest when needed. But it also frees you. It frees you from seeking divinity outside of yourself. It teaches you that awakening is not a destination — it is a daily devotion.

When meditation becomes a way of life, your entire existence becomes a ceremony. And from that place, you no longer need to escape the world to find peace — you carry peace into the world, embodied and alive.

You are the practice.
You are the presence.
You are the temple.
And that is more than enough.

Becoming the Meditation

A Final Transmission for the Journey Ahead
This book has been a doorway — one of many — into the sacred art of meditation. But words eventually fall away. Scripts fade. Techniques dissolve. And what remains is not the method, but the memory — the remembrance that you are not separate from what you seek.

You are not merely a student of meditation. You are its embodiment. Its expression. Its living echo.

You Are the Portal
There will come a moment — perhaps subtle, perhaps seismic — when you realize that you no longer need to "do" meditation in order to be connected. You will wake up and feel the sacred in your bones. You will walk outside and hear the earth speak in the rustle of leaves. You will listen to a friend in pain and feel your own heart pulse in theirs.

This is the turning point. The moment where the inner temple becomes inseparable from your everyday life. Where your nervous system becomes a tuning fork for peace, and your energy field becomes a sanctuary for others.

You are the portal now. To stillness. To safety. To remembrance. When you close your eyes, you do not disappear — you expand. When you guide another, you do not lead — you open space for their own divine unfolding.

Carrying the Torch
If you are reading this as a practitioner, guide, or future facilitator, know this: your work matters. Your voice matters. Your presence changes lives.

In a world of noise, you are cultivating silence. In a culture of disconnection, you are teaching embodiment. In a time of fear, you are anchoring light.

You are carrying an ancient flame — passed from mystic to mystic, teacher to seeker, soul to soul. Let it burn in your heart. Let it illuminate the path for others. Let it guide you when you forget. You do not need to be perfect. You only need to be true. True to your breath. Your body. Your knowing.

As we close, I invite you to pause. To breathe. To bring your hands to your heart and feel the pulse of your own sacred rhythm.

Ask yourself: What is awakening in me? What wants to be remembered? What am I ready to embody?

Breathe into the answers. Let them rise not from thought, but from the soul. Let them activate a frequency — unique to you — that will continue to ripple long after these pages are closed.

You are not alone. You are not behind. You are exactly where you need to be.

May your path be blessed. May your voice be clear. May your presence be medicine.

And may you remember — again and again — that you are the meditation. You are the blessing. You are the light.

And the world is ready for you.

Dear Reader,

Thank you — truly — for walking this path with me. Whether you are a seeker, a teacher, a practitioner, or simply someone curious about the power of meditation, I honor the courage it takes to turn inward. In a world that constantly pulls us outward, the choice to slow down, to listen, and to remember your inner wisdom is a radical act of healing.

This book was born not just from study, but from my lived experience — from trauma and transformation, from silence and song, from nights when I wasn't sure I'd make it through, and mornings when I remembered why I was here. It is my hope that these pages have offered you both inspiration and practical support. That somewhere in this text, you've found not just information — but resonance.

To those of you who will bring these practices into your healing rooms, classrooms, or circles: thank you for being stewards of the sacred. You are the next wave of guides, helping others return to themselves. May your work be grounded in integrity, compassion, and presence.

To those meditating alone on their living room floor, seeking connection with the Divine in their own way — your practice matters just as deeply. You are part of a greater field of consciousness rising.

And to those whose nervous systems have been hurt in places where "healing" was supposed to happen — may this book remind you that your body is not broken, your sensitivity is not weakness, and your truth is welcome here.

Thank you for your time, your heart, and your willingness to engage with this work. May it continue to serve you long after the last page is turned.

In devotion,
Chelsey Sarah Prusha, B.Msc.

Appendix: Meditation Styles by Origin and Purpose

This appendix is designed as a quick-reference guide to the many meditation styles explored throughout this book. Organized by origin and purpose, it provides an accessible overview of diverse practices, their roots, and how they can be applied in personal or professional settings.

INDIAN (VEDIC/HINDU) ORIGIN

Mantra Meditation
Purpose: Focus and spiritual attunement through repetition.
Origin: Vedic tradition (India)
Effectiveness: Calms the mind and aligns consciousness with sound vibration.
How Used: Silent or vocal repetition of a mantra (e.g., "Om," "So Hum").

Transcendental Meditation (TM)
Purpose: Access deep rest and pure awareness.
Origin: Maharishi Mahesh Yogi (Modern Vedic)
Effectiveness: Scientifically studied for stress reduction and creativity.
How Used: 15–20 minutes twice daily with a personal mantra.

Yoga Nidra (Yogic Sleep)
Purpose: Deep relaxation, subconscious reprogramming.
Origin: Ancient Tantric texts
Effectiveness: Induces a hypnagogic state for healing and inner exploration.
How Used: Guided body scan and visualization in savasana.

Chakra Meditation
Purpose: Energetic alignment and spiritual awakening.
Origin: Tantra, Vedic Yoga
Effectiveness: Balances subtle body systems.
How Used: Visualizing energy centers, colors, sounds, or deities.

BUDDHIST ORIGIN

Vipassana (Insight Meditation)
Purpose: Clear-seeing into the nature of reality.
Origin: Theravāda Buddhism
Effectiveness: Cultivates equanimity and detachment from cravings.
How Used: Noting sensations, thoughts, and breath without attachment.

Metta (Loving-Kindness Meditation)
Purpose: Cultivate compassion for self and others.
Origin: Buddhist Sutta teachings
Effectiveness: Increases empathy and emotional

regulation.
How Used: Repeating phrases of goodwill to self, then others.

Zazen (Seated Zen)
Purpose: Observe pure presence, "just sitting."
Origin: Zen Buddhism (China/Japan)
Effectiveness: Builds mindfulness, discipline, and ego dissolution.
How Used: Sitting in silence, often facing a wall, observing breath and posture.

Tonglen (Giving and Taking)
Purpose: Transform pain into compassion.
Origin: Tibetan Buddhism
Effectiveness: Trains the heart to open in difficulty.
How Used: Inhale suffering, exhale love and healing.

DAOIST / CHINESE ORIGIN

Qi Gong Meditation
Purpose: Harmonize and circulate life force (Qi).
Origin: Daoist practices
Effectiveness: Strengthens vitality, grounds the nervous system.
How Used: Breath, posture, and slow movement or visualization.

Inner Smile & Microcosmic Orbit
Purpose: Nourish internal organs with positive

energy.
Origin: Taoist Alchemy
Effectiveness: Balances emotions and internal meridian flow.
How Used: Visualize smiling into each organ; circulate energy through meridian loop.

JEWISH / CHRISTIAN / SUFI / MYSTICAL ORIGINS

Contemplative Prayer
Purpose: Deep communion with the Divine.
Origin: Christian Mysticism (Desert Fathers, Teresa of Ávila)
Effectiveness: Fosters spiritual intimacy and surrender.
How Used: Silent repetition of sacred words (e.g., "Jesus," "God is Love").

Kabbalistic Meditation
Purpose: Unite with divine light and cosmic order.
Origin: Jewish mysticism
Effectiveness: Invokes spiritual awakening through sacred names and symbols.
How Used: Meditation on Hebrew letters, divine names, Tree of Life.

Sufi Whirling / Dhikr
Purpose: Ecstatic union with the Divine.
Origin: Sufi Islam
Effectiveness: Dissolves ego through rhythmic trance

and divine remembrance.
How Used: Chanting divine names (dhikr) or physical spinning (whirling dervishes).

MODERN / WESTERN / NEUROSCIENTIFIC

Mindfulness-Based Stress Reduction (MBSR)
Purpose: Reduce stress and increase presence.
Origin: Jon Kabat-Zinn (1979, USA)
Effectiveness: Scientifically validated for anxiety, pain, depression.
How Used: Body scan, mindful breathing, awareness of sensations and thoughts.

Guided Visualization
Purpose: Intentional imagery for healing or manifestation.
Origin: Western psychology, shamanic roots
Effectiveness: Stimulates neuroplasticity, emotional regulation.
How Used: Audio or live guide leads a journey (e.g., inner child, future self).

Hypnotherapy/Trance Meditation
Purpose: Reprogram subconscious beliefs.
Origin: Western psychology and esoteric hypnosis
Effectiveness: Fast-tracks behavior change and inner healing.
How Used: Inductions, affirmations, inner dialogue in relaxed theta state.

INDIGENOUS / EARTH-BASED

Shamanic Journeying
Purpose: Access spirit worlds, healing, soul retrieval.
Origin: Global indigenous traditions
Effectiveness: Facilitates personal transformation, ancestral connection.
How Used: Drumbeat or rattle to induce altered states; guided inner travels.

Nature-Based or Elemental Meditation
Purpose: Reconnect with Earth and elements.
Origin: Animist and indigenous practices
Effectiveness: Grounds energy, soothes the body, opens intuitive channels.
How Used: Meditating with trees, fire, water, wind, stones.

ENERGETIC / ASCENSION-BASED (NEW EARTH)

Light Code / DNA Activation
Purpose: Awaken multidimensional potential and soul memory.
Origin: Starseed & Ascension teachings
Effectiveness: Expands awareness, recalibrates the energy field.
How Used: Light language, vocal tones, channeling cosmic energy.

Merkaba or Sacred Geometry Meditation
Purpose: Activate light body and divine blueprint.
Origin: Egyptian/Kabbalistic fusion
Effectiveness: Strengthens spiritual protection and quantum navigation.
How Used: Visualizing spinning geometric fields (e.g., tetrahedrons, Metatron's cube).

About the Author

Chelsey Sarah Prusha, B.Msc., is a multidimensional healer, clinical hypnotherapist, spiritual teacher, and meditation guide devoted to helping others reclaim their inner truth and embody their soul's wisdom. With a background in Western healthcare and over a decade of experience in healing, Chelsey is the founder of The Synergy Wellness Collective, creator of Rainbow Reiki Advanced Energy Healing, and the visionary behind Trinity Wellness Therapy.

A survivor of complex trauma, addiction, misdiagnosis, and spiritual disconnection, Chelsey's personal journey from fragmentation to embodiment has shaped every aspect of her work. As an AuDHD mother, energy intuitive, and trauma-informed guide, she weaves together the science of the subconscious with the sacredness of the soul — offering grounded tools for healing and expansive pathways to transformation.

Chelsey's work bridges ancient wisdom and modern modalities, fusing meditation, metaphysics, hypnosis, energy medicine, and sacred ritual into multidimensional systems of care. Her meditations are not just techniques, but transmissions — designed to open hearts, awaken consciousness, and restore connection to the divine self.

Through this book and her greater body of work, Chelsey offers a gentle yet powerful invitation: to remember who you are beneath the noise, and to become the Living Temple of your own sacred existence.

www.ingramcontent.com/pod-product-compliance
Lightning Source LLC
Chambersburg PA
CBHW052057230426
43662CB00037B/2012